THE FIVE SEASONS KITCHEN

PIERRE GAGNAIRE

THE FIVE SEASONS KITCHEN

PIERRE GAGNAIRE

| *90 simple and creative recipes* |

Photographer Jacques Gavard | *Food stylist Sabrina Fauda-Rôle*

GRUB STREET • LONDON

A few months before the anniversary marking my 50th year in cooking, my loved ones, who had long been asking me to write a family cookbook, finally won me over. The idea behind this book is to make something simple: simple, of course, refers to the products used, but also to the process. No stock, no sauce, no cooking or assembly method is overly convoluted; no fancy equipment is required for any of the components.

Whenever there is a weekend or holiday approaching that will allow me to catch up with friends and loved ones, I naturally feel invested in the catering…

This great responsibility is one I accept with pleasure and joy, because in the end it is what I do best. I leave tasks like fixing power cuts and repainting the shutters to my wife: I am creative, true, but as far as DIY goes I am hopeless.

What makes being gathered around the dinner table such a pleasant experience? First of all, it's the effort that goes into the shopping. Even if the raw materials are modest, care must be taken to find the best leek, the best olive oil, the best cut of meat. Of course, we don't always have time to browse for the sake of browsing, but having a close relationship with the merchant can make such a difference. It's the effort that goes into the table setting, which doesn't necessarily have to be pretentious: rather, it consists of striking the appropriate tone for the event. Essentially, the time spent in the kitchen is that precious time when, between the delicious aromas and the division of labour, the feeling of a community reunited already begins to take shape.

■ ■ ■

As I grow older, I appreciate this time in suspension, with its almost choreographic rhythm. I would not have been able to write this collection of recipes twenty years ago; for me back then, cooking had to express an artistic concept, a unique and challenging idea. None of that features in this book: only an attempt to provide, over the course of these five seasons, a few personal ideas for a generous and immediate cuisine.

Why five seasons?

The fifth season is that moment after winter has ended but before spring has truly begun. Each year there is a ray of sunlight, a change in the wind, an emerging bud, a feeling of renewal marking the end of the cold; and yet nature still has nothing to offer. But the chef in me has to try, even faced with the scarcity of the marketplace, to express this idea of renewal; to bid farewell to the cabbages, artichokes, salsify and root vegetables.

Cooking is not measured in terms of modernity or tradition, you understand: the only real requirement is that the cook's loving care is evident.

I would be remiss not to thank Michel Nave in particular, my loyal colleague of 35 years; he has grown alongside me and has managed to find his own voice on my playing field. We complement each other, and this is expressed in this book: I created the recipes and Michel put them into practice.

This cookbook aims only to give a few starting points for a delicious, light, dedicated and hassle-free way of cooking.

PIERRE GAGNAIRE TT

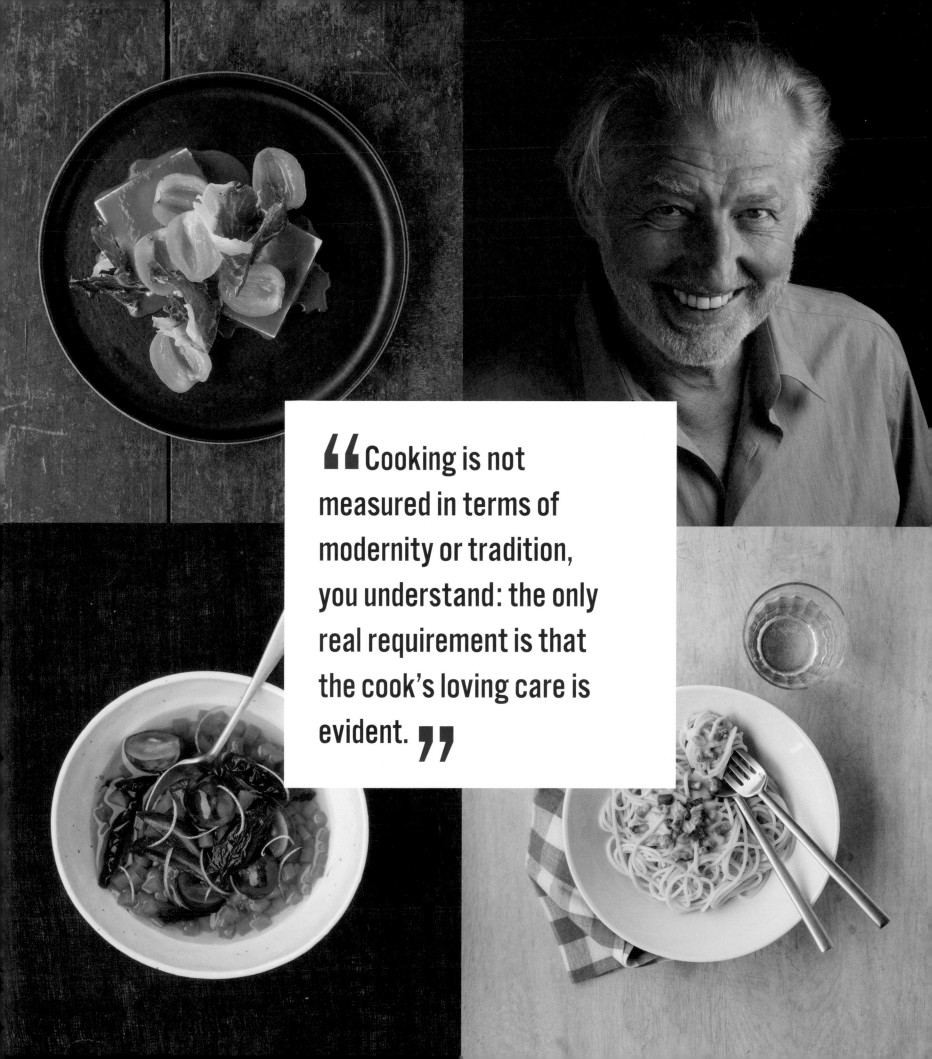

"Cooking is not measured in terms of modernity or tradition, you understand: the only real requirement is that the cook's loving care is evident."

SUMMARY OF
CONTENTS

⊤⊤

MENUS

WINTER

Almost SPRING

True SPRING

SUMMER

AUTUMN

APPENDICES

MENUS

WINTER

December | January | February

WINTER

MENU
01

| STARTER | MAIN | DESSERT |

Puy green lentil soup
with foie gras

Shimizu chicken supreme
with avocado, pink grapefruit,
green apple and celery

Butternut squash, Medjool dates
and fresh grapes infused in cinnamon syrup

WINTER

MENU
02

| STARTER | MAIN | DESSERT |

Pearl barley,
spinach and plankton

Slice of duck foie gras
with oysters

Rum-soaked savarin,
blood orange and Thai grapefruit

WINTER

MENU
03

| STARTER | MAIN | DESSERT |

Chicory stuffed with dried apricots and golden raisins,
served with a Parmesan cream sauce

Sliced fillet of doe with black pepper, juniper,
radicchio mousseline and turmeric crisps

Victoria pineapple
with saffron and kirsch

WINTER

MENU 04

| *page 32* |

| STARTER | MAIN | DESSERT |

Parsnip velouté with Mostarda di Cremona
and bitter leaves

Leg of Veal Pot-au-feu with star anise,
thick sweet potato stock,
red cabbage and Comice pear

Chestnut cream with marc de Côtes-du-Rhône
and burst blackcurrants

WINTER

MENU 05

| *page 38* |

| STARTER | MAIN | DESSERT |

Coffee-scented chestnut velouté
with fluffy egg whites and mortadella

Lamb shoulder rubbed with curry leaf,
einkorn wheat, dried figs and pine nuts

Infusion of dragon fruit,
rambutans, mangosteens and clementines

WINTER

MENU 06

| *page 44* |

| STARTER | MAIN | DESSERT |

Tarbais beans,
cockles and jambon de Paris

Crisp roast pollack with
tandoori mashed potatoes
and caramelised apples

Lemon tuiles
with pink grapefruit jelly

WINTER

MENU
01

STARTER

Serves 6

30 g butter

½ onion, chopped

70 g smoked bacon lardons

1 clove garlic, peeled

1 bouquet garni (green leek
   leaves wrapped around a few
   stalks of parsley, 1 sprig of thyme
   and 1 bay leaf)

For the lentil soup

250 g green lentils

1 litre vegetable stock (or 1 litre water)

Fine salt and freshly ground black pepper

250 g duck foie gras,
   thickly sliced

PREPARATION TIME | *20 minutes*

COOKING TIME | *30 minutes*

Puy green lentil soup
with foie gras

Method

1 FOR THE LENTILS
Sweat the onion and the bacon lardons in the butter. Add the garlic, the bouquet garni and the lentils. Pour in the vegetable stock, bring to the boil, skim off any froth and leave to cook gently.

2 FOR THE FOIE GRAS
Season the slices of foie gras with salt and quickly pan fry.

3 FOR THE SOUP
Remove the bouquet garni from the lentils and drain, reserving the stock. Process ¾ of the lentils with the foie gras in a blender, adding a little of the cooking stock to obtain a creamy texture. Next, strain through a chinois. Combine this soup with the remaining lentils and season with salt and pepper if required.

Finishing

Serve in a soup bowl. This soup can be served with clementine segments, celeriac and croutons.

MENU
01

MAIN

Serves 6

6 free-range chicken breasts (supremes)

For the marinade

3 cloves garlic, crushed

100 ml olive oil + extra for frying

50 ml mirin

250 ml sweet, fortified white wine
(Rivesaltes AOC)

10 g curry leaves or fresh thyme

1 tbsp paprika

3 celery stalks, peeled
and cut into 2–4 cm dice

2 pink grapefruits, peeled and supremed

Knob fresh butter

3 avocados, peeled, stones
removed and roughly diced

1 green apple, cut into
brunoise (dice)

Bunch plucked fresh coriander leaves

Salt and freshly ground white pepper

Tip

Marinate the chicken breasts for
24 hours in the garlic, olive oil, mirin,
white wine and curry leaves.

PREPARATION TIME | *30 minutes*

COOKING TIME | *25 minutes*

Shimizu chicken supreme
with avocado, pink grapefruit, green apple and celery

Method

1 FOR THE CHICKEN SUPREMES
Season the chicken breasts, then sear quickly in olive oil (3 minutes). Add the marinade and the paprika and simmer gently, covered, for 10 minutes.

2 FOR THE CELERY
Boil the celery in salted water for 2 minutes, then cool in cold water and drain.

3 FOR THE MARMALADE
Cook the grapefruit segments and juice with the butter for 5 minutes. Leave to cool, then add the avocados, green apple and celery. Return to a low heat for a few seconds.

Finishing

Divide the grapefruit, avocado and apple marmalade between the plates, then top with the sliced chicken breasts and their jus. Sprinkle with fresh coriander leaves.

WINTER

MENU
01

DESSERT

Serves 6

500 ml still mineral water

150 g granulated sugar

1 cinnamon stick

300 g butternut squash,
   cut into small dice

200 g red grapes, halved

12 Medjool dates, pitted
   and chopped

Zest and juice of 1
   unwaxed lime

Lime or passion fruit sorbet
   (optional)

Butternut squash, Medjool dates
and fresh grapes infused in cinnamon syrup

Method

1 **FOR THE SYRUP**
Bring the water to the boil in a saucepan with the sugar and cinnamon. Leave to infuse until completely cooled. Remove the cinnamon stick.

2 **FOR THE SQUASH**
Place the squash in a saucepan, cover completely with cold syrup and bring to the boil, then remove from the heat and leave to cool completely (the squash should yield easily when pressed with a finger).

3 **FOR THE FRUIT SALAD**
Combine the grapes with the dates and the squash in its syrup. Add the lime zest and juice to the fruit salad. Chill before serving.

Finishing

Serve in a large bowl, perhaps with a layer of crisp puff pastry or an exotic sorbet.

Serves 6

40 ml olive oil

1 red onion, finely diced

1 clove garlic, minced

1 lemon, peeled and supremed

300 g pearl barley, boiled in salted water

200 ml vegetable stock

100 g double cream

½ tsp powdered plankton
   (found in organic shops)

200 g spinach, chopped

1 tbsp chives, chopped

Salt and freshly ground white pepper

PREPARATION TIME | *20 minutes*

COOKING TIME | *10–15 minutes*

Pearl barley,
spinach and plankton

Method

1 **FOR THE ONION FONDUE**
Sweat the red onions in the oil, but do not allow to brown. Season, add the garlic and the lemon segments and cook for 2–3 minutes. Remove.

2 **FOR THE PEARL BARLEY**
Heat the pearl barley with the vegetable stock for 5–6 minutes, then add the cream and plankton. Return to the boil and add the spinach and chives. Combine the onion fondue with the green barley mixture. Season to taste.

Finishing

Divide the pearl barley between 6 deep dishes while still hot and retaining its deep green colour.

Serves 6

6 x 40–50 g slices raw
duck foie gras

Flour (as needed, for coating)

18 Brussels sprouts, rinsed

Olive oil

60 g butter

Pinch mild curry powder

2 grey griselle shallots, chopped

18 medium spéciale oysters (size 3,
50 g; ask the fishmonger to shuck
them if you wish)

20 ml Manzanilla sherry
or high-quality sauvignon blanc

8 thin slices Morteau sausage, cut into
matchsticks

2 tbsp brioche breadcrumbs
mixed with 2 tbsp grated
Beaufort cheese

Salt

PREPARATION TIME | *25 minutes*

COOKING TIME | *15 minutes*

Slice of duck foie gras
with oysters

Method

1 FOR THE FOIE GRAS
Flour the slices of foie gras, fry quickly, then place on kitchen paper
and season lightly with salt.

2 FOR THE BRUSSELS SPROUTS
Boil the Brussels sprouts in salted water, then leave to cool and pat
dry. Cut the sprouts in half and use to colour the olive oil by placing them
cut-side down in the frying pan.

3 FOR THE OYSTERS
Heat the butter with the curry powder in a fairly large frying pan until
bubbling, then quickly brown the shallots. Next, add the oysters and cook
for 30 seconds, then remove from the heat, deglaze with the Manzanilla
sherry and drain.

4 FOR THE MORTEAU SAUSAGE
Heat the sausage matchsticks briefly in a frying pan without oil.

Finishing

Divide the Morteau sausage between six deep dishes and add the foie
gras, Brussels sprouts and the oysters with their cooking liquid. Divide
the breadcrumb and Beaufort mixture between the dishes. When
serving, take care to ensure that both the dish and the ingredients are
hot enough to allow the Beaufort to melt slightly.

MENU
02

DESSERT

Serves 6

For the savarin

4 egg yolks

160 g sugar

260 g plain flour + extra for the mould

180 g butter, melted and cooled
  + extra for the mould

20 g baking powder

4 egg whites, whisked into firm peaks

For the rum syrup

500 ml still mineral water

200 g brown sugar

1 vanilla pod, halved

Peel of 4 oranges, removed using a peeler

100 ml golden rum

For the citrus salad

4 blood oranges, peeled
  and supremed

120 g Thai grapefruit flesh,
  separated into vesicles

50 ml grenadine

PREPARATION TIME | *30 minutes*

COOKING TIME | *30 minutes*

Rum-soaked savarin,
blood orange and Thai grapefruit

Method

1 FOR THE SAVARIN
Preheat the oven to 180°C, 350°F, gas 4. Whisk the yolks and sugar together until the mixture turns pale. Add the flour and combine gently. Add the melted butter and the baking powder, combine until smooth, then add the stiff egg whites without breaking the texture. Transfer to a greased and floured 20-cm savarin mould. Bake for 20 minutes, then lower the oven temperature to 150°C, 300°F, gas 2 and bake for a further 8 minutes. Leave to cool, then remove from the mould.

2 FOR THE RUM SYRUP
Heat the water with the sugar, vanilla and orange peel. Leave to cool before adding the rum.

3 TO SOAK THE SAVARIN
Place the savarin in a deep dish (this will be the serving dish) and ladle the warm syrup over the top, one ladleful at a time: the syrup should soak all the way through to the middle.

4 FOR THE ORANGE AND GRAPEFRUIT FRUIT SALAD
Combine the orange segments and their juice with the Thai grapefruit and grenadine. Refrigerate.

Finishing

Place the fruit salad in the centre of the savarin and serve. The savarin can be served with sweet whipped cream (Chantilly) flavoured with a hint of rum and orange zest, or with vanilla ice cream.

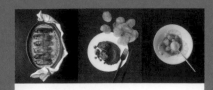

MENU
03

STARTER

Serves 6

6 heads of chicory, all of the same grade

Juice of 1 lemon

60 g fresh butter
 + extra for the filling and for frying

Pinch sugar

1 shallot, chopped

6 dried apricots, diced

30 g golden raisins, soaked
 in water and drained

1 tbsp breadcrumbs

12 chives, scalded

500 ml double cream

120 g Parmesan, grated

2 tbsp Noilly Prat® vermouth

Fine salt and freshly ground white pepper

PREPARATION TIME | *30 minutes*

COOKING TIME | *50 minutes*

Chicory stuffed
with dried apricots and golden raisins, served with a Parmesan cream sauce

Method

1 **FOR THE BRAISED CHICORY**
Preheat the oven to 180°C, 350°F, gas 4. Arrange the chicory in a casserole dish and fill the dish with water and lemon juice until half submerged. Add the diced butter and the sugar and season lightly with salt. Cover with baking paper and bring to a low boil. Place the lid on top and transfer to the oven for 30–40 minutes. Check that they are cooked by piercing with a knife: if it slides in easily, they are ready. Drain and leave to cool. Next, open the chicory out flat and remove some of the flesh from the centre.

2 **FOR THE APRICOT AND RAISIN FILLING**
Brown the shallot in the butter, chop the chicory hearts and add, then cook until they release their water. Remove from the heat, then add the apricots, raisins and breadcrumbs. Season and mix together.
Divide the filling between the chicory heads, roll up and secure with a few knotted chives. Melt a little butter until brown, then use to colour the chicory.

3 **FOR THE PARMESAN CREAM SAUCE**
In a saucepan, reduce the cream by half, then add the Parmesan and Noilly. Season with salt and pepper if required.

Finishing

Preheat the oven to 160°C, 325°F, gas 3. Transfer the Parmesan cream sauce to a gratin dish, place the chicory on top and bake in the oven for 10 minutes.

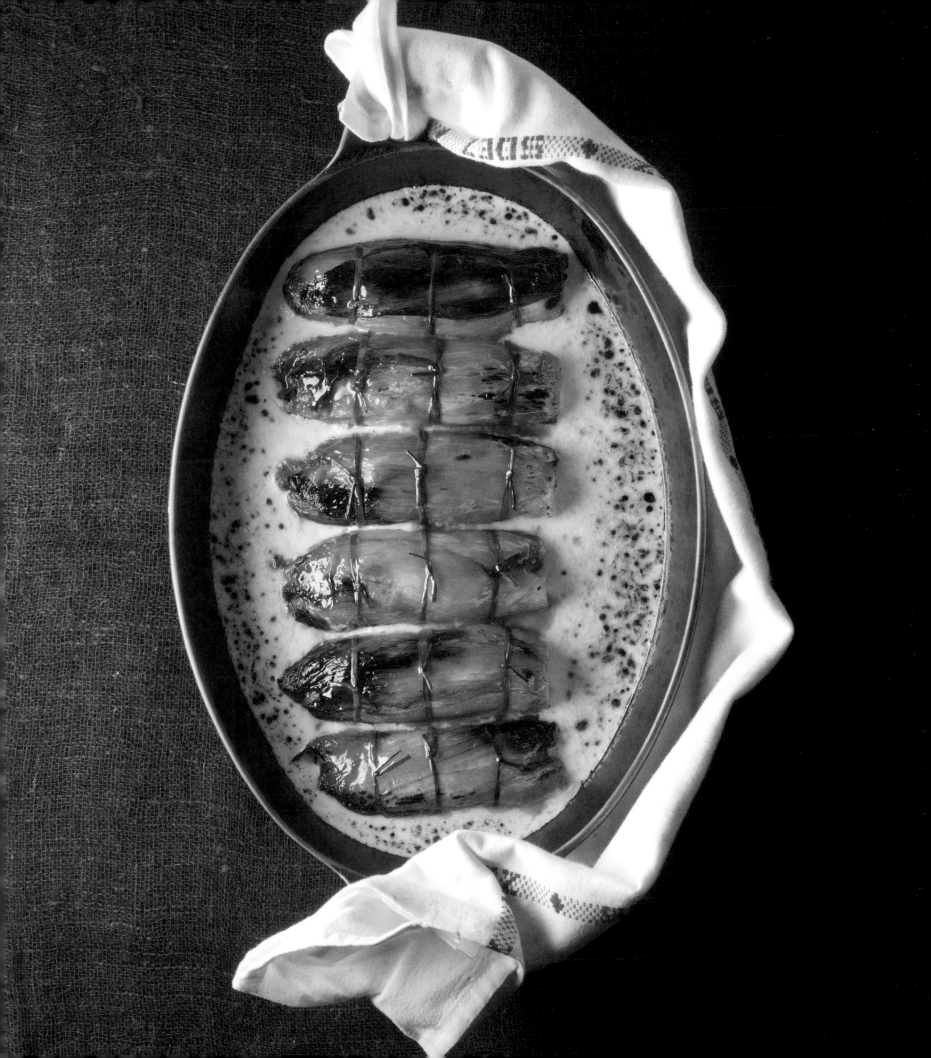

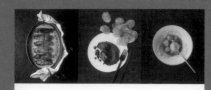

WINTER

MENU
03

MAIN

Serves 6

1 kg medium-sized Bintje
   potatoes, peeled and sliced
   using a mandoline

1 tbsp turmeric

6 slices doe fillet
   (110 g each, bones and nerves removed)

2 tbsp crushed black peppercorns

4 juniper berries, crushed

Olive oil

100 g fresh butter

1 head radicchio, chopped
   (Italian chicory)

20 ml sherry vinegar

20 ml hazelnut oil

Fine salt

Peanut oil or margarine

PREPARATION TIME | *30 minutes*

COOKING TIME | *20 minutes*

Sliced fillet of doe
with black pepper, juniper, radicchio mousseline and turmeric crisps

Method

1 ONE DAY IN ADVANCE
Place the potatoes in an ice bath seasoned with turmeric and set aside for 24 hours. Season the slices of doe fillet with pepper, crushed juniper and a few spoonfuls of olive oil 24 hours before cooking.

2 FOR THE RADICCHIO MOUSSELINE
Heat the butter in a saucepan until it froths, then cook the radicchio. Season lightly with salt. Deglaze the pan with the vinegar. Process the radicchio with care, then add the hazelnut oil.

3 FOR THE SLICES OF DOE FILLET
Just before cooking, season lightly with salt and quickly sear in olive oil for 3 minutes, then finish in a clean frying pan: heat the butter until frothing, then add the doe fillets. Leave to rest in the hot pan.

4 FOR THE CRISPS
Remove the potato slices dyed with turmeric from their bath and carefully pat dry. Fry under close supervision until crisp and completely golden. Drain on paper towels.

Finishing

Place the radicchio mousseline in the centre of each plate and place a slice of doe fillet on top. Divide the crisps between 6 bowls. The crisps can be served with small slices of bacon, fried until crunchy.

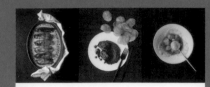

Serves 6

1 large Victoria pineapple,
    skin carefully removed

High-quality kirsch

250 g granulated sugar

Saffron strands

PREPARATION TIME | *15 minutes*

COOKING TIME | *5 minutes*

Victoria pineapple
with saffron and kirsch

Method

1 FOR THE PINEAPPLE SLICES
Cut 6 thin slices from the pineapple. Cover with kirsch and 50 g of the sugar, then leave to macerate for 2 hours.

2 FOR THE SAFFRON CUBES
Remove the hard core from the remaining pineapple and cut the flesh into large chunks. Fry with the remaining caster sugar and a few strands of saffron. Leave to cool.

Finishing

Divide the saffron pineapple chunks between 6 deep dishes and place a macerated slice directly on top, without draining. Serve this dessert with pineapple sorbet, passion fruit sorbet or a sweet mâche salad.

WINTER

MENU
04

STARTER

Serves 6

500 g parsnips, peeled and chopped

750 ml milk

60 g butter

100 g Mostarda di Cremona (found in specialist spice shops)

Nutmeg

2 crimson (red) chicories, chopped

120 g radicchio di Treviso, chopped

120 g green frisée lettuce, chopped

2 grey griselle shallots, chopped

3 tbsp walnut oil

1 tbsp white balsamic vinegar

Salt and freshly ground black pepper

PREPARATION TIME | *15 minutes*

COOKING TIME | *30 minutes*

Parsnip velouté
with Mostarda di Cremona and bitter leaves

Method

1 FOR THE PARSNIP VELOUTÉ
Cook the parsnips in the milk (slightly salted) for 30 minutes. Drain, reserving the milk, then process together with the fresh butter. Add the milk from the cooking to obtain a somewhat pale velouté.
Drain the fruits from the mostarda and finely chop. Add to the cream of parsnip along with the mostarda syrup, then grate in some nutmeg.

2 FOR THE LEAVES
Combine the 3 types of leaf in a large salad bowl with the shallots. Season with walnut oil, white balsamic vinegar, salt and pepper. Mix together.

Finishing

Divide the mixed leaves between six deep dishes, and serve the velouté separately. The velouté can be served with blood sausage.

MENU 04

MAIN

Serves 6

1 large boneless hind leg of veal (cleaned and tied by the butcher)

For the garnish
1 bouquet garni
2 onions, chopped
1 large leek, chopped
6 carrots, chopped
White part of 3 leeks
2 sticks celery, peeled
2 star anises
1 level tbsp coarse salt

1 small sweet potato, finely diced
Dash rapeseed oil
Knob fresh butter
¼ red cabbage, chopped
20 ml sherry vinegar
4 gherkins, finely diced
2 tbsp capers
1 large, ripe pear,
peeled and finely diced
40 g fresh butter
250 ml high-quality Riesling wine
Fine salt and freshly ground black pepper

PREPARATION TIME | *35 minutes*

COOKING TIME | *2 hours*

Leg of Veal Pot-au-feu
with star anise, thick sweet potato stock, red cabbage and Comice pear

Method

1 FOR THE LEG OF VEAL
Place the leg of veal and garnish in a high-sided pot or casserole, then fill with cold water until fully immersed. Add the coarse salt and bring to the boil. When the water starts to boil, use a small ladle to skim any froth from the top. Leave to simmer gently for approximately 1 hour 30 minutes. Remove the leg and strain the stock. Reduce if necessary. Allow for 250 ml stock per person.

2 FOR THE SWEET POTATO
Cook the sweet potato in the stock from the leg of veal. Process and strain the stock, add the rapeseed oil and the butter. The stock obtained should be fluid, almost liquid.

3 FOR THE RED CABBAGE
Pour the hot vinegar over the cabbage. Add the gherkins, capers and pear to the cabbage and fry quickly in the butter: the cabbage should remain crunchy. Season with salt and pepper.

Finishing

Cut the leg into generous slices and place in a casserole dish. Drizzle with Riesling, cover and bring to the boil, then serve immediately in the casserole dish. The red cabbage and hot stock are served separately.

MENU
04

DESSERT

Serves 6

400 g chestnut cream

30 ml marc de Côtes du Rhône

250 ml whipped cream

250 g frozen blackcurrants

200 g sugar

2 tbsp crème de cassis liqueur

PREPARATION TIME | *15 minutes*

COOKING TIME | *4–5 minutes*

Chestnut cream
with marc de Côtes-du-Rhône and burst blackcurrants

Method

1 **FOR THE CHESTNUT CREAM**
Process with the marc and gently fold in the whipped cream. Freeze.

2 **FOR THE CRÈME DE CASSIS**
Place the blackcurrants in a small saucepan with the sugar and cook briskly until the berries have all burst. Leave to cool, then add the crème de cassis.

Finishing

Divide the blackcurrant mixture between six deep dishes, then add the frozen chestnut cream. This dessert can be served with coffee ice cream, candied kumquats or even a few black truffle shavings if desired.

WINTER

MENU
05

STARTER

Serves 6

600 g fresh chestnuts,
    peeled and raw

1 litre milk

100 g fresh butter

1 cup espresso

4 egg whites

6 thin slices mortadella,
    cut into strips

Salt and freshly ground white pepper

PREPARATION TIME | *20 minutes*   **COOKING TIME** | *1 hour*

Coffee-scented chestnut velouté
with fluffy egg whites and mortadella

Method

1 **FOR THE COFFEE-SCENTED CHESTNUT VELOUTÉ**
Cook the chestnuts in the milk, lightly salted, for 1 hour. Drain, reserving the milk, and reduce the chestnuts to a purée. Season. Thin the purée with the hot milk, then process, adding the butter and the coffee, until a creamy soup–like texture is obtained.

2 **FOR THE FLUFFY EGG WHITES**
Whip the egg whites into stiff peaks with a pinch of salt. Use a spoon to create 18 quenelles of egg whites, then poach one by one in simmering water for 2–3 minutes, turning occasionally. Set aside on paper towels.

Finishing

Divide the chestnut velouté between six deep dishes, then add three quenelles of egg white to each and scatter the mortadella on top. This velouté can be served with diced, grilled pork or roast chicken.

Serves 6

1 x 1.8–2 kg lamb shoulder,
   boned and tied by the butcher
4 sprigs curry leaf or fresh thyme
Peel of 2 oranges, removed using a peeler
Peel of 2 lemons, removed using a peeler
1 white onion, chopped
2 shallots, thickly sliced

Olive oil
8 cloves garlic, whole and unpeeled
200 ml dry white wine
Salt

250 g einkorn wheat
3 tbsp Ricard® pastis
50 g butter
8 dried figs, finely chopped
50 g toasted pine nuts
2 lemons, quartered (optional)

PREPARATION TIME | *25 minutes*

COOKING TIME | *2 hours 45 minutes*

Lamb shoulder
rubbed with curry leaf, einkorn wheat, dried figs and pine nuts

Method

1 ONE DAY IN ADVANCE
Marinate the lamb shoulder with the curry leaf, citrus peel, onion and shallots for 24 hours.

2 TO COOK THE LAMB SHOULDER
Preheat the oven to 200°C, 400°F, gas 6. Remove the shoulder from the marinade, clean, season with salt and brown in a frying pan with some olive oil.
Meanwhile, in a casserole with a lid, gently brown the onion, garlic and shallot for 10 minutes. Place the shoulder on top and roast in the oven for 20 minutes. Pour over the white wine and roast for a further 15 minutes. Cover, reduce the heat to 150°C, 300°F, gas 2 and cook gently for 1 hour 30 minutes, regularly adding spots of water, until a knife pierces the meat easily and the garnish is juicy and caramelised.

3 FOR THE EINKORN WHEAT
Bring a pot of lightly salted water to the boil and add a dash of Ricard®, then cook the einkorn wheat for 30–50 minutes. Drain, drizzle with sizzling butter, then add the dried figs and toasted pine nuts.

Finishing

Carve the lamb shoulder and serve in deep dishes with the vegetables from the braising. Serve the einkorn wheat separately, accompanied by lemon quarters if desired.

WINTER

MENU
05

DESSERT

Serves 6

1 dragon fruit

500 ml water

400 g sugar

1 vanilla pod, cut in
half lengthways

6 clementines, supremed
with each segment cut into thirds

18 rambutans, peeled and diced

12 mangosteens, peeled
and diced

PREPARATION TIME | *15 minutes*

COOKING TIME | *3 minutes*

Infusion of dragon fruit,
rambutans, mangosteens and clementines

Method

ONE DAY IN ADVANCE

Peel the dragon fruit without discarding the skin. Cut the skin into strips and the flesh into small dice. Boil a pan with the water, sugar, vanilla and dragon fruit skin. Leave to infuse until completely cooled. Strain and add the remaining fruit. Leave to infuse for 24 hours before serving.

Finishing

Serve the fruit infusion in individual bowls or large ramekins. Can be accompanied by rice pudding or thick slices of mango.

Serves 6

For the beans

300 g Tarbais beans
(from this year if possible), soaked for
24 hours in cold water (or pochas, cooked
white Spanish beans in jars)

100 g smoked bacon

1 tbsp caraway seeds, sealed
in a teabag (or, failing this, use juniper)

Fine salt

For the cockles

Knob butter

2 shallots, chopped

100 ml dry white wine

1 clove garlic, minced

600 g cockles, carefully
washed and rinsed

150 ml intense olive oil
(with strong flavour)

2 tbsp Dijon mustard

3 tbsp chestnut honey

1 tbsp crushed black peppercorns

180 g jambon de Paris,
finely diced

PREPARATION TIME | *30 minutes*

COOKING TIME | *1 hour 45 minutes*

Tarbais beans,
cockles and jambon de Paris

Method

1 TO COOK THE BEANS
Cook the Tarbais beans in the smoked bacon in a saucepan over a low heat (1 hour 30 minutes). Next, add the bag of caraway seeds and some salt. Remove the caraway seeds and the bacon, and leave to cool.

2 TO COOK THE COCKLES
Brown the shallots in the fresh butter. Add the white wine, garlic and cockles and cook, covered, for 5–8 minutes, stirring regularly. Leave to cool, then drain and remove the cockles from their shells. Strain the liquid carefully to remove any sand. Reduce this liquid with 50 g of the Tarbais beans, then process, adding the olive oil and the mustard.
Heat the ham with the honey and the black pepper until bubbling.

Finishing

Combine the drained Tarbais beans, cockles and jambon de Paris with the cooking liquid. Divide the lard between 6 warmed cups, then pour over the warm bean stew.

MENU
06

MAIN

Serves 6

6 pollack steaks, skin on
(120 g each)

For the mash

1.5 kg Bintje potatoes, peeled and diced

1 tsp tandoori spice mix

Fresh butter

200 ml milk

200 ml crème fraîche

For the apples

2 Royal Gala apples, peeled
and cut into thin segments

Granulated sugar

Chickpea flour

Olive oil

Juice of 1 lemon

Fine salt and freshly ground black pepper

PREPARATION TIME | *35 minutes*

COOKING TIME | *30 minutes*

Crisp roast pollack
with tandoori mashed potatoes and caramelised apples

Method

1 FOR THE MASHED POTATOES
Boil the potatoes in salted water, drain and mash with a fork. Add the tandoori spices and the butter. Combine the milk with the cream, bring to the boil and add to the mash.

2 FOR THE CARAMELISED APPLES
Cook the apples in sizzling butter, then sprinkle with sugar and continue cooking until caramelised.

3 FOR THE POLLACK
Roll the pollack steaks skin-side down in the chickpea flour, then tap to remove any excess. Cook skin-side down in a non-stick frying pan with the olive oil. Once the skin is crisp and golden, remove the fish and wipe the pan clean. Finish off by cooking again in sizzling butter (3 minutes), then deglaze the pan with lemon juice. Season with salt and pepper.

Finishing

Place 1 tablespoon of mashed potato on each of 6 large plates, then add the apple segments, one pollack steak and the cooking butter. Serve the remaining mash separately.

WINTER

MENU
06

DESSERT

Serves 6

4 pink grapefruits, supremed,
 reserving both skin and juice

130 g granulated sugar
 + extra for the marmalade
 to be weighed out during cooking

5 g gelatine leaves, soaked
 in cold water

150 g still mineral water

2 individual yoghurts (30% fat)

20 g crushed ice

For the tuiles

60 g icing sugar + extra
 for finishing

30 g T55 flour

1 egg white

30 g melted butter

Grated zest of ¼ lemon

Juice of 1 lemon

Pinch citric acid

PREPARATION TIME | *30 minutes*

COOKING TIME | *2 hours 30 mins approx.*

Lemon tuiles
with pink grapefruit jelly

Method

1 FOR THE GRAPEFRUIT JELLY
Process the grapefruit segments and juice, then strain. Weigh out 300 g of this liquid, reserving the rest, then bring ¼ of it to the boil and add the sugar. Wring out the gelatine leaf and add. Next, add the remaining ¾ of the grapefruit juice to the hot liquid containing the gelatine. Leave to cool. Transfer the cool liquid to deep dishes and refrigerate.

2 FOR THE YOGHURT AND THE FROZEN GRAPEFRUIT JUICE
Recover the remaining grapefruit juice and process along with the yoghurt and the crushed ice.

3 FOR THE CANDIED GRAPEFRUIT MARMALADE
Dice the grapefruit skins evenly. Blanch three times (boil in 3 separate pans of water, one after the other, starting from cold each time). Drain, weigh the skins and add the same weight in sugar. Simmer gently in a heavy-bottomed saucepan with a little water for 1½–2 hours. Add a little water during cooking if necessary. Leave to cool.

4 FOR THE LEMON TUILES
Preheat the oven to 180°C, 350°F, gas 4. Combine the icing sugar with the flour, add the egg white and then the melted and cooled butter. Finally, add the lemon zest and juice. Brush out discs 12 cm in diameter onto lined baking sheets. Bake for 7–8 minutes. Remove the warm tuiles from the baking paper. Store in a dry place.

Finishing

Divide the candied grapefruit marmalade between the plates of jelly. Sprinkle the tuiles with icing sugar seasoned with citric acid and serve on the plates or separately. The grapefruit yoghurt is served in frosted glasses.

MENUS

Almost

SPRING

March | *April*

Almost
SPRING

MENU
07

| STARTER | MAIN | DESSERT |

Chopped scallops
in lemon-scented orange sugar,
served with avocado tao

Pork filet mignon flavoured with vadouvan
and served with fondant potatoes and prunes

Apple slivers "à la Juliette"

Almost
SPRING

MENU
08

| STARTER | MAIN | DESSERT |

Broccoli with brown shrimp butter

Haddock rounds and bluefin tuna tartare
with beetroot syrup

Chocolate soup with nut crumble

Almost
SPRING

MENU
09

| STARTER | MAIN | DESSERT |

Bouchot mussels with lemon balm
and cauliflower slices

Roast beef
with 6 rue de la Pépinière sauce

Sweet wine and lime infusion
with pear, mango, lychee and pomegranate

Almost
SPRING

**MENU
10**

| *page 72* |

| STARTER | MAIN | DESSERT |

**Vegetable consommé
with lemongrass and ginger,
served with shredded vegetables**

Blanquette de veau

Orange tart

Almost
SPRING

**MENU
11**

| *page 78* |

| STARTER | MAIN | DESSERT |

Sole terrine with leek

**De Cecco® n°7 spaghetti
with onion and Gorgonzola cream**

**Joconde sponge cake with meringue,
grappa sabayon and Granny Smith julienne**

Almost
SPRING

**MENU
12**

| *page 84* |

| STARTER | MAIN | DESSERT |

Healthy soup

**Turmeric fried monkfish
with lemon and caper relish**

**Three little pots-de-crème:
vanilla, coffee and chocolate**

Serves 6

18 scallops, diced

Juice of 2 oranges

Juice of 1 lemon

Potato starch

2 avocados, peeled, stoned
and chopped

Juice of 1 lime

150 g crushed ice or ice cubes

4 tbsp condensed milk

50 g fresh butter

Salt and Espelette pepper

PREPARATION TIME | *15 minutes*

COOKING TIME | *5–10 minutes*

Chopped scallops
in lemon-scented orange sugar,
served with avocado tao

Method

1 FOR THE ORANGE SUGAR
Reduce the orange juice by half over a low heat, then add the lemon juice, return to the boil, add a little potato starch to thicken until it can coat the back of a spoon.

2 FOR THE AVOCADO TAO
Purée the avocados with the lime juice, crushed ice and condensed milk. Season with salt and Espelette pepper.

3 FOR THE SCALLOPS
Heat the butter in a frying pan until bubbling and warm the seasoned scallops but do not allow them to cook. Remove from the heat, add the orange sugar and mix well to coat the scallops.

Finishing

Place a tablespoon of cold avocado tao in the bottom of each dish, then divide the warm scallops between them.

Almost
SPRING

MENU
07

MAIN

Serves 6

1 kg pork filet mignon

2 sweet onions, diced

1 shallot, chopped

2 pinches vadouvan
(found in Indian spice shops)

4–5 potatoes cut into 18 slices,
each 1.5 cm thick

Fresh butter

Salt and ten pink peppercorns

18 prunes, soaked in 500 ml apple juice

Pork filet mignon
flavoured with vadouvan and
served with fondant potatoes and prunes

Method

1 FOR THE FILET MIGNON
Preheat the oven to 200°C, 400°F, gas 6. Heat the butter in a roasting tin and brown the filet mignon on all sides. Roast for around 10 minutes. Add the onions, shallot and vadouvan, then cook for a further 15 minutes. Next, cover, lower the oven to 150°C, 300°F, gas 2 and leave to braise for approximately 40 minutes. Remove the meat and keep warm. Purée the onion and shallot with the meat juices.

2 FOR THE FONDANT POTATOES AND PRUNES
Preheat the oven to 180°C, 350°F, gas 4. Arrange the potato circles in a large gratin tray. Drain the apple juice from the prunes and pour it over the potatoes until fully immersed, then add a few pieces of butter and season with salt and crushed pink peppercorns. Cover with baking paper and bake, adding the prunes halfway through (after approximately 20 minutes). Continue baking until the potatoes can be easily pierced with a knife (you may need to add more liquid during cooking).

Finishing

Finely slice the filet mignon and serve on plates over the onion and vadouvan coulis. Serve the fondant potatoes in the gratin tray in the centre of the table. This dish can be accompanied by a salad of pigs' ears.

Almost
SPRING

MENU
07

DESSERT

Serves 6

3 Royal Gala apples, peeled,
    halved and seeds removed
60 g brown sugar
Fresh butter
100 ml apple juice
    (failing this, use mineral water)
6 slices brioche
100 ml milk
1 egg
20 g granulated sugar
3 tbsp redcurrant jam

PREPARATION TIME | *20 minutes*

COOKING TIME | *45 minutes*

Apple slivers
"à la Juliette"

Method

1 **FOR THE APPLES**
Preheat the oven to 180°C, 350°F, gas 4. Thinly slice each apple half (as you would for an apple tart) and place in a gratin tray, pressing down gently on each one to loosen the slices and aid cooking. Sprinkle with brown sugar, place a few knobs of butter on top of the apples and moisten with apple juice. Cover with aluminium foil and bake for 15 minutes. Remove the foil and cook for a further 10–15 minutes, basting well to glaze. Leave to cool in the gratin tray.

2 **FOR THE FRENCH TOAST**
Combine the milk, egg and sugar. Soak each slice of brioche in this mixture and brown both sides in butter in a non-stick frying pan. Warm the redcurrant jam, whisking gently until fluid.

Finishing

Serve the apples warm in their gratin tray. Place a slice of French toast on each plate and drizzle with redcurrant jam. Invite the guests to top their French toast with the apple à la Juliette.

Serves 6

200 g whole brown shrimp

250 ml still mineral water

2 heads broccoli

Coarse salt

80 g fresh butter

Potato starch

Salt and freshly ground black pepper

PREPARATION TIME | *20 minutes*   COOKING TIME | *15 minutes*

Broccoli with brown shrimp butter

Method

1 FOR THE SHRIMP INFUSION
Shell the shrimp completely, set aside the flesh in the refrigerator and place the heads and shells in a saucepan. Toast gently without oil. Add the water and leave to infuse for approximately 15 minutes, covered, over a very low heat. Do not allow to boil. Allow to cool completely, then strain.

2 FOR THE BROCCOLI
Separate the heads from the stalks; leave the heads whole. Boil the heads in salted water, then halt the cooking process by immersing in iced water, handling with caution as broccoli is fragile when cooked. Peel the stalks, cut into brunoise and boil in salted water.

3 FOR THE BROWN SHRIMP BUTTER
Measure out 200 ml of shrimp infusion, bring to the boil and thicken slightly with the potato starch. Next, process along with small cubes of butter. Add the peeled shrimp tails and the broccoli brunoise. Set aside in a bain marie over a low heat.

Finishing

Serve the warm broccoli heads and the brown shrimp butter separately, the latter in a large sauce boat.

Serves 6

1 haddock fillet

300 g bluefin tuna fillet,
    finely diced

2 Agria potatoes, boiled
    and pressed through a strainer

30 g crème fraîche

1 raw beetroot,
    peeled and grated

250 ml still mineral water

10 ml sherry vinegar

Potato starch

2 tsp soy sauce

10 ml sesame oil

20 ml olive oil

1 tbsp chives, chopped

1 tsp black sesame seeds

Tabasco® sauce

Fine salt and freshly ground white pepper

PREPARATION TIME | *30 minutes*

COOKING TIME | *10 minutes*

Haddock rounds
and bluefin tuna tartare with beetroot syrup

Method

1 **FOR THE HADDOCK ROUNDS**
Preheat the oven to 200°C, 400°F, gas 6. Cut thin escalopes from the haddock fillet (as you would for smoked salmon). Place side-by-side on a sheet of baking paper and bake for 2 minutes. Cut out six 8-cm circles from this layer of haddock. Reserve these haddock rounds and the scraps left over.

2 **FOR THE HADDOCK PURÉE**
Combine the haddock scraps, the potato purée and the crème fraîche. Keep warm.

3 **FOR THE BEETROOT SYRUP**
Combine the grated beetroot and the mineral water. Bring to the boil and infuse for 15 minutes, covered, in a warm place. Press the beetroot through a strainer, extracting as much juice as possible. Return to the heat and reduce by half, add the sherry vinegar, season lightly with salt and thicken with the starch to create a deep red, sticky syrup (it should coat the back of a spoon).

4 **FOR THE TARTARE**
Combine the tuna with the soy sauce, sesame oil, olive oil and chives. Finally, add the black sesame seeds and the Tabasco® (to taste). Transfer loosely to 5-cm square moulds, without pressing or forcing. Refrigerate.

Finishing

Mould the warm haddock purée into round discs, then top with the warm haddock rounds and the cube of tuna tartare in the centre. Drizzle with beetroot syrup to complete the dish.

Almost
SPRING

MENU
08

DESSERT

Serves 6

For the chocolate water
250 ml still mineral water
50 g granulated sugar
25 g cocoa powder
14 g gelatine leaves, soaked
　in cold water

For the chocolate soup
200 ml double cream
450 ml whole milk
400 g dark chocolate, broken up

For the nut crumble
100 g unsalted butter, softened
　(left out at room temperature)
100 g granulated sugar
100 g ground hazelnuts
100 g T55 flour
100 g chopped walnuts

PREPARATION TIME | *20 minutes*　　　COOKING TIME | *20 minutes*

Chocolate soup
with nut crumble

Method

1 FOR THE CHOCOLATE WATER
Boil the water with the sugar. Remove from the heat and add the cocoa. Wring out the gelatine and add. Pour into a baking dish to approximately 1.5 cm thick. Leave to harden in the refrigerator, then cut into cubes.

2 FOR THE CHOCOLATE SOUP
Boil the cream with half of the milk, then gradually pour over the chocolate, whisking together. Once the mixture is smooth and consistent, add the remaining milk. Leave to cool completely.

3 FOR THE NUT CRUMBLE
Preheat the oven to 160°C, 325°F, gas 3. Rub the softened butter into the sugar, ground hazelnut, flour and chopped walnuts to a coarse crumble. Spread this crumble out over a silicone sheet and bake for approximately 15 minutes. Leave to cool.

Finishing

Divide the cubes of chocolate water between six dishes, then pour the cold soup on top and finish with small chunks of nut crumble.

Serves 6

4 kg bouchot mussels, cleaned

4 shallots, chopped

Fresh butter

3 stalks lemongrass, chopped

500 ml dry white wine (sauvignon blanc)

½ cauliflower, separated into florets and sliced finely using a mandoline

50 g crème fraîche

30 g coconut milk

10 g lemon balm leaves, chopped (or flat-leaf parsley)

2 tbsp kirsch

Fine salt

PREPARATION TIME | *20 minutes*   COOKING TIME | *15 minutes*

Bouchot mussels
with lemon balm and cauliflower slices

Method

1 FOR THE MUSSELS
Sweat the shallots in a large saucepan with some fresh butter and the lemongrass but do not allow them to brown. Add the white wine and bring to the boil, then add the mussels and stir. Cover and cook until the shells open. Transfer to a colander to catch the cooking liquid, then filter through a cloth and return to the heat to reduce by ⅓. Remove the mussels from their shells and remove the lemongrass and shallots.

2 FOR THE CAULIFLOWER
Boil the cauliflower slices for 1 minute in salted water, then drain and leave to dry without refreshing under water. Brown in the butter in a non-stick frying pan.

3 FOR THE MUSSEL LIQUID
Add the crème fraîche and the coconut milk to the reduced mussel liquid, bring to the boil, then process and add the kirsch.

Finishing

Divide the hot mussels between six deep dishes, dress with the sauce, add the cauliflower and sprinkle with the chopped lemon balm.

Almost
SPRING

MENU
09

MAIN

Serves 6

For the sauce

1 red onion, chopped

½ red pepper + ½ green pepper,
 peeled and diced

2 tomatoes, peeled,
 seeded and chopped

½ pink grapefruit, peeled
 and supremed

1 carrot, finely diced
 and boiled in salted water
 but still crunchy

Peel of 3 lemons,
 removed using a peeler

½ tsp caraway seeds

1 tsp vadouvan spice mix

2 g mace

100 g strawberries, hulled and chopped

125 g raspberries

50 g raw beetroot, peeled
 and finely chopped

20 ml sherry vinegar

80 g brown sugar

Olive oil

1 fresh sage leaf

8 fresh mint leaves

30 g redcurrants

Salt and cayenne pepper

1.8 kg beef for roasting (sirloin, for example),
 prepared and tied by the butcher

40 g butter

40 g sunflower oil

Fine salt and freshly ground black pepper

PREPARATION TIME | *35 minutes*

COOKING TIME | *45 minutes*

Roast beef
with 6 rue de la Pépinière sauce

Method

1 FOR THE SAUCE
Sweat the onion and peppers in olive oil for 5–10 minutes but do not allow to brown. Next, add the remaining ingredients (except the sage, mint and redcurrants). Cook over a low heat for 30 minutes, stirring regularly. Season lightly with salt.

Add the sage and mint, then cook for approximately 10 more minutes. Leave to cool, then process in a blender to a creamy sauce. Add the redcurrants, then season to taste with salt and pepper.

2 TO COOK THE BEEF
Preheat the oven to 240°C, 475°F, gas 9. Season the meat with salt and then sear in olive oil in a very hot pan. Remove from the pan and finish cooking in the oven on a pre-heated baking tray with some fresh butter (15 minutes). Baste the meat regularly, and add a few spoonfuls of water if necessary to prevent the butter from burning. Remove the meat from the oven, wrap in aluminium foil and leave to rest for 20 minutes.

Finishing

Season the hot meat with pepper and place on a serving platter. Serve the sauce separately. Serve this dish with a baked potato and a crisp romaine lettuce salad.

Serves 6

4 Comice pears, diced

1 mango, finely diced

2 bananas, finely diced

100 g brown sugar

Grated zest and supremed
   segments of 2 limes

180 g fresh lychees, pitted and cut
   into aiguillettes (long strips)

Seeds of ½ pomegranate

200 ml sweet wine (Muscat)

PREPARATION TIME | *15 minutes*

COOKING TIME | *2 minutes*

Sweet wine and lime infusion
with pear, mango, lychee and pomegranate

Method

1 **FOR THE FRUIT SALAD**
Combine the pears, mango and bananas and season with the sugar, lime zest and chopped lime segments. Refrigerate for around 2 hours.

2 **FOR THE SWEET WINE**
Heat the wine and leave to cool. Combine the pomegranate seeds and the lychees with the rest of the fruit. Pour the wine over the fruit salad.

Finishing

Serve the fruit salad chilled. Accompany with an almond biscuit, if desired.

Serves 6

For the consommé

150 g carrots, peeled
and finely chopped

150 g celery, finely chopped

150 g white mushrooms, cleaned
and finely chopped

150 g leek, cleaned
and finely chopped

100 g turnip, peeled
and finely chopped

150 g fennel

10 g stick lemongrass, crushed

50 g fresh ginger, peeled and minced

1.5 litres still mineral water

1 teabag or muslin bag filled with 2 g black
pepper, 2 g coriander seeds and 2 slices of
lemon peel, removed using a peeler

Fine salt

For the shredded vegetables

30 g carrot, julienned

30 g celery, julienned

30 g leek (white part only), julienned

30 g turnip, cut into matchsticks

20 g chives, cut into matchsticks

White balsamic vinegar

Sesame oil

Fine salt

PREPARATION TIME | *25 minutes*

COOKING TIME | *5–10 minutes*

Vegetable consommé
with lemongrass and ginger, served with shredded vegetables

Method

1 **FOR THE CONSOMMÉ**
Place all of the vegetables, the water and the teabag in a large saucepan, season lightly with salt and bring to the boil. Turn off the heat and cover the saucepan with food wrap so it is airtight, then leave to infuse very slowly over a low heat for around 1–1½ hours. Strain through a chinois, pressing the vegetables gently.

2 **FOR THE SHREDDED VEGETABLES**
Mix together all of the shredded vegetables and season.

Finishing

Divide the shredded vegetables between six deep dishes and pour over the consommé at the table. This dish can also be served chilled. It can be accompanied by kefir, noodles or macaroni.

Almost
SPRING

MENU
10

MAIN

Serves 6

500 g boneless leg of veal,
   cut into chunks

500 g boneless veal belly,
   cut into chunks

2 carrots, cleaned and cut into chunks

1 leek, cleaned and cut into chunks

1 white onion, halved
   and studded with one clove

2 celery stalks, cut into chunks

2 litres still mineral water

150 g butter

50 g flour, sieved

Juice of 1 lemon

180 g white button mushrooms, cleaned

180 g pearl onions

Sugar

200 ml double cream

2 egg yolks

Fine salt, coarse sea salt
   and freshly ground black pepper

PREPARATION TIME | *40 minutes*

COOKING TIME | *1 hour 40 minutes*

Blanquette de veau

Method

1 TO COOK THE MEAT
Place the meat, carrots, leek, white onion and celery in a casserole and cover with water, add a little coarse salt and bring to a low boil. Carefully skim off any foam and simmer gently for at least 1 hour. The meat is cooked when it is tender and can be pierced easily.

2 FOR THE ROUX
Meanwhile, heat 50 g of the butter in a small saucepan until sizzling, then add the flour and cook over a low heat for 5 minutes, stirring with a whisk. Transfer to a separate container and leave to cool.

3 FOR THE MUSHROOMS AND PEARL ONIONS
Wipe clean the roux pot and boil 100 ml water with 50 g of the butter and the lemon juice, then add the mushrooms and season with a little salt. Cook, stirring, for 6 minutes. Place the onions in a single layer in a wide pan, then add the final 50 g butter and one pinch each of coarse salt and sugar, then pour over the water until immersed. Cover with baking paper and cook gently, stirring, until all of the liquid has evaporated.

4 FOR THE SAUCE AND TO COMPLETE THE BLANQUETTE
Drain and reserve the meat. Strain the stock, heat until reduced to approximately 500 ml. While still boiling, thicken the stock by gradually adding the cold roux, stirring well with the whisk. Add the cream, bring to the boil and thicken. Next, add the meat, vegetables, mushrooms and onions and simmer for 10 minutes. Remove a little of the sauce and combine with the egg yolks. Mix it all together and serve immediately.

Finishing

Serve the blanquette in the casserole with the garnish. Can be accompanied by a ginger-scented basmati rice pilaf or a pea, lettuce and spring onion salad.

Almost
SPRING

MENU
10

DESSERT

Serves 6–8

You will need a circular tart tin 24 cm in diameter

For the sweet pastry
120 g butter
80 g icing sugar
25 g ground almonds
½ tsp sea salt
Seeds of 1 vanilla pod
200 g flour
1 egg

For the orange segments
200 g orange segments
4 g pectin NH
Sugar

For the bitter orange marmalade
4 untreated oranges
170 g sugar
120 ml water
½ tsp ginger powder

For the orange cream
500 ml orange juice
Juice of 2 lemons
90 g caster sugar
4 eggs
10 g orange zest
2 gelatine leaves
120 g bitter orange marmalade
100 g butter

PREPARATION TIME | *35 minutes*

COOKING TIME | *2 hours 30 minutes*

Orange tart

Method

1 FOR THE SWEET PASTRY
Work the butter into a silky paste. Add the icing sugar, mix, then add the other ingredients one by one. Finish with the egg. Let the dough rest for 1 hour in the refrigerator, then roll it 3–4 mm thick. Line the bottom and the sides of the tart tin with the dough and bake at 160°C, 325°F, gas 3 for 12 minutes.
Cut the excess dough around the edges once the pie has cooled.

2 FOR THE ORANGE SEGMENTS
Cut each of the orange segments into three. Boil the orange pieces with the pectin and a little sugar. Refrigerate.

3 FOR THE BITTER ORANGE MARMALADE
Wash the oranges and cook whole in a pan filled with boiling water for about 30 minutes. Drain and cool the fruit in running water for 15 minutes. Cut slices and reserve the juice in a container.
Keep a quarter of slices and chop the rest into small dice.
Make a syrup with the sugar and water. Once the temperature reaches 115°C, 239°F, add reserved orange juice and heat to 112°C, 234°F. Pour the syrup over the chopped oranges,
sprinkle with ginger and cook gently for 30 minutes, stirring often. Refrigerate.

4 FOR THE ORANGE CREAM
Reduce the orange juice down to 100 ml. Mix the reduced orange juice, lemon juice, sugar, eggs and zest in a pan. Bring to a boil, then add the gelatine. Let it cool to 50°C, 122°F and mix with the orange marmalade and butter. Leave the cream to rest for 1 hour to cool.

Finishing

When the orange cream is very cold pour it over the cooled pastry base, decorate with reserved orange slices. Serve the orange segments apart or sprinkle on the tart.

MENU
11

STARTER

Serves 6

½ onion, chopped

1 shallot, chopped

1 sprig thyme

1 bay leaf

500 ml dry white wine

400 ml still mineral water

2 small 300 g soles,
   gutted and heads removed

6 gelatine leaves,
   soaked in cold water

2 leeks (white part only), cleaned and
   chopped

Olive oil

1 tbsp capers in vinegar,
   crushed with the flat of a knife

10 confit tomato petals, diced

Salt and freshly ground black pepper

PREPARATION TIME | *40 minutes*   COOKING TIME | *45 minutes*

Sole terrine
with leek

Method

1 **TO PREPARE THE COURT-BOUILLON AND THE SOLES**
Combine the onion, shallot, thyme, bay leaf, white wine and water in a casserole pot. Season lightly with salt and simmer for 15 minutes. Strain, pressing the vegetables to release their juices. Preheat the oven to 110°C, 225°F, gas ¼. Transfer the court-bouillon to a baking dish, immerse the soles so that they lie flat, and bake for 10–15 minutes. Drain and remove the skin while still warm, then separate into 8 fillets.

2 **FOR THE JELLY**
Filter the sole cooking liquid through a cloth, then transfer to a pan and reduce to 500 ml. Dissolve the soaked gelatine in the liquid. Adjust the seasoning as necessary.

3 **FOR THE TANGY VEGETABLE MIXTURE**
Sweat the leeks in a dash of olive oil and a little water. Leave to cool. Combine the cooked leek, the capers and the confit tomato in a large bowl.

4 **TO ASSEMBLE THE TERRINE**
The assembly of the terrine consists of stacking the different ingredients with the jelly in between. Pour a jelly base 0.5 cm thick into the bottom of a terrine mould and leave to set in the refrigerator. Next, place the sole fillets, cover with a little more jelly and leave to set. Place the vegetable mixture on top, then some jelly, leave to set, and so on until the mould is full. Once complete, leave overnight to firm up completely in the refrigerator before unmoulding.

Finishing

Serve the terrine on a dish, cut into slices, with a fresh vegetable salad.

Serves 6

180 g smoked bacon lardons
100 g fresh butter
3 sweet onions, chopped
250 ml double cream
150 g Gorgonzola cheese
600 g De Cecco® no. 7 spaghetti
Coarse salt and pepper

PREPARATION TIME | *15 minutes*

COOKING TIME | *25 minutes*

De Cecco® no. 7 spaghetti
with onion and Gorgonzola cream

Method

1 FOR THE ONION AND GORGONZOLA CREAM
Sauté the bacon in a saucepan with 30 g butter, then remove with a slotted spoon and set aside. In the same pan, sweat the onions for 10 minutes in the bacon fat (do not add salt). Add the cream, cover and cook for 15 minutes over a low heat. Process, adding the Gorgonzola in pieces. Combine the onion cream with the lardons and keep warm.

2 TO COOK THE SPAGHETTI
Bring a pot of salted water (8 g coarse salt per litre) to the boil and add the spaghetti. Cook at a rolling boil, uncovered, until al dente. Heat the remaining butter in a separate pan until bubbling, then strain the pasta, rinse briefly with a little boiling water and add the sizzling butter.

Finishing

Serve the spaghetti on a dish, separate from the onion and Gorgonzola cream. This dish can be served with grilled calamari or a tomato soup.

Almost
SPRING

MENU
11

DESSERT

Serves 6

For the Joconde sponge cake
90 g eggs (2 eggs)
50 g icing sugar
70 g ground almonds
60 g egg whites (2 whites)
15 g granulated sugar
20 g T55 flour
15 g melted butter

For the meringue
100 g egg whites (3 large whites)
100 g granulated sugar

For the grappa sabayon
4 egg yolks
150 g granulated sugar
30 ml grappa

For the Granny Smith julienne
Juice of 1 lemon
2 Granny Smith apples,
   julienned

PREPARATION TIME | *25 minutes*

COOKING TIME | *20–30 minutes*

Joconde sponge cake
with meringue, grappa sabayon and Granny Smith julienne

Method

1 FOR THE JOCONDE SPONGE CAKE
Preheat the oven to 180°C, 350°F, gas 4. Whisk together the whole eggs, icing sugar and ground almonds. Whisk the egg whites with the granulated sugar until soft peaks form, then fold gently into the whole egg mixture, taking care that they do not collapse. Add the flour and melted butter. Transfer to a non-stick cake tin and bake for approximately 12 minutes, using the tip of a knife to check if they are ready. Once out of the oven, remove from the mould and transfer to a cooling rack.

2 FOR THE MERINGUE
Prepare a bain marie at around 60°C, 140°F (the water should be just starting to bubble). Use an electric beater to mix the egg whites with the sugar, then place the container in the bain marie and continue to beat continuously at a high speed until the meringue batter turns clear and swells (it should reach a temperature of 45–50°C, 113–122°F). Remove from the bain marie and continue beating until cooled completely. The finished meringue batter should be very white, smooth and firm. Transfer to a piping bag fitted with a wide, fluted nozzle.

3 FOR THE GRAPPA SABAYON AND THE GRANNY SMITH JULIENNE
Combine the egg yolks with the sugar and the grappa using an electric beater. Place the container in a bain marie (identical to the one used for the meringue batter) and continue to beat until smooth, firm and mousse-like. Remove from the bain marie and beat until cooled completely. Combine the lemon juice with the julienned apple.

Finishing

Cut the Joconde cake into slices and pipe out the meringue on top. Use a blowtorch (or a crème brûlée iron) to brown the meringue. Place the Joconde sponge cake on plates and divide the apple julienne between them. Serve the sabayon separately in the centre of the table. This dessert can be served with a green apple and coriander granita or lime sorbet.

Almost
SPRING

MENU
12

STARTER

Serves 6

4 large leeks, cleaned
Fresh butter
1 Agria potato, peeled and diced
1.5 litres still mineral water
6 slices sandwich bread, crusts removed
Sunflower oil
250 ml whipped cream, seasoned
Salt and freshly ground white pepper

PREPARATION TIME | *20 minutes*

COOKING TIME | *20–25 minutes*

Healthy soup

Method

1 FOR THE SOUP
Separate the white and green parts of the leek. Chop the whites, sweat in the butter and season lightly with salt. Add the potato, pour in the mineral water and bring to the boil, then leave to simmer, covered, until the potato is completely cooked. Process in a blender, then strain through a chinois, modify the seasoning and texture as required and set aside in a bain marie.

2 FOR THE LEEK FONDUE
Chop very finely only the softest of the green leek leaves. Sweat gently in fresh, salted butter until very tender. Set aside in a warm place.

3 FOR THE CROUTONS
Dice the bread. Brown in a frying pan with a dash of oil. Set aside on paper towels and keep warm.

Finishing

Divide the leek fondue among 6 deep dishes, then pour over the hot soup. Finish with 1 tablespoon of cold whipped cream. Serve the croutons in a separate serving dish.

Serves 6

For the monkfish

1 x 800 g monkfish fillet, cleaned
    and ready for use
1 tsp turmeric
5 tbsp olive oil
1 clove garlic, finely minced
Fresh butter
Dash lemon juice

For the lemon relish

2 unwaxed lemons, quartered
100 g granulated sugar
250 ml pineapple juice, strained
100 ml grapefruit juice, strained
80 g short-grain rice, boiled in salted water
1 tbsp capers, chopped
1 small tsp tarragon, chopped
50 g celery, finely diced
Juice of 1 lemon
Fine salt and freshly ground white pepper

PREPARATION TIME | *30 minutes*

COOKING TIME | *3 hours 10 minutes*

Turmeric fried monkfish
with lemon and caper relish

Method

1 FOR THE LEMON RELISH
Blanch the lemon quarters three times by immersing them in cold water and bringing to the boil. Remove the seeds, cook for 3 hours with the pineapple and grapefruit juices and the sugar (if necessary, add a little mineral water during cooking). Leave to cool completely, drain, then chop the candied lemons.

Combine the rice with the capers, tarragon and celery, then add to the lemon relish. Season with salt and pepper as needed and sharpen with fresh lemon juice as desired.

2 FOR THE MONKFISH
Cut the monkfish fillet into 18 pieces. Combine the turmeric, olive oil and garlic. Season the pieces of monkfish with this mixture. Marinate for 1 hour in a cool place.

Quickly brown the monkfish pieces in a non-stick frying pan. Season with salt and leave to rest for 5–10 minutes. Heat again for 2–3 minutes in sizzling butter, then deglaze with a dash of lemon juice.

Finishing

Just before serving, halve the pieces of monkfish and place on a very hot dish. Serve the monkfish and the lemon relish separately. The monkfish can be accompanied by a few wilted spinach leaves or steamed potatoes.

Almost
SPRING

MENU
12

DESSERT

Serves 6

For the vanilla crème

8 egg yolks

100 g granulated sugar

750 ml milk

1 vanilla pod, halved

For the coffee crème

8 egg yolks

100 g sugar

750 ml milk

20 ml coffee extract or
very strong espresso

For the chocolate crème

8 egg yolks

175 g sugar

750 ml milk

40 g bitter cocoa powder

PREPARATION TIME | *20 minutes*   COOKING TIME | *25 minutes*

Three little pots-de-crème:
vanilla, coffee and chocolate

Method

1 **FOR THE VANILLA CRÈME**
Preheat the oven to 180°C, 350°F, gas 4. Whisk the eggs yolks and sugar together until the mixture turns pale. Bring the milk to the boil with the vanilla, then pour the hot milk over the egg yolks, stirring. Leave to rest,
then transfer to pots or ramekins, skimming any mousse from the surface if necessary. Line a roasting tin with baking paper and place the pots on top, then fill the tin with boiling water until the pots are half-submerged. Cook, covered, for around 25 minutes. The surface of the crème should be smooth, shiny and slightly wobbly. Leave to cool for 50–60 minutes.

2 **FOR THE COFFEE CRÈME**
Repeat the same recipe, replacing the vanilla with coffee extract.

3 **FOR THE CHOCOLATE CRÈME**
The recipe remains the same: take care to ensure that the cocoa powder dissolves completely.

Finishing

The little pots should be served as is, chilled, with a few sablé biscuits, little meringues or warm brioche.

MENUS

True

SPRING

May | June

True

SPRING

MENU

13

| *page 94* |

| STARTER | MAIN | DESSERT |

Zézette soup

Meat Pithivier

Caramelised pear brunoise with coconut bavarois and muscovado tuiles

---

True

SPRING

MENU

14

| *page 100* |

| STARTER | MAIN | DESSERT |

Eggs à la Berrichonne

Sienna langoustines
with enokitake amaranth

Financiers with rocket chlorophyll
and mint syrup

True

SPRING

MENU

15

| *page 106* |

| STARTER | MAIN | DESSERT |

Green pea velouté
with Sauternes cubes and baby vegetables

Red mullet with Bellino stuffing

Red berry salad
with melted lavender honey
and white balsamic vinegar

True

SPRING

MENU
16

| *page 112* |

| STARTER | MAIN | DESSERT |

Maharajah cauliflower

Grilled sea bass
with chopped rocket, semi-brined anchovy
and cabbage

Rhubarb tart
with apricot coulis

True

SPRING

MENU
17

| *page 118* |

| STARTER | MAIN | DESSERT |

Steak and smoked eel tartare
with salted radish

Croaker fish in craft cider
served with Camembert, watercress and mange tout

Chocolate Armagnac soufflé
with toasted flour sablé biscuits

True

SPRING

MENU
18

| *page 124* |

| STARTER | MAIN | DESSERT |

White mushrooms
in Colombo-style mustard sauce,
served with squid rings

Grilled salmon steak flavoured
with blonde beer, molasses and nuoc-mâm,
served with sorrel and raspberry fondue

Pan-fried Burlat cherries
with brown sugar and Zan®,
served with Amaretto cherry syrup

Serves 6

800 g fresh white mushrooms, chopped

140 g fresh butter

250 ml dry white wine (sauvignon blanc)

750 ml still mineral water

2 tbsp soy sauce

200 ml sweet white wine (Muscat)

250 g coconut cream

2 cloves garlic, crushed

10 g fresh flat-leaf parsley

10 g fresh coriander

10 g chives

10 g chervil

1 tbsp Savora® mustard

Salt and Espelette pepper

6 slices sandwich bread, toasted

PREPARATION TIME | *30 minutes*

COOKING TIME | *50–55 minutes*

Zézette soup

Method

1 FOR THE ZÉZETTE SOUP
Sauté the mushrooms in 40 g of the butter but do not allow to brown. Season lightly with salt. Add the dry white wine and the water, bring to the boil and add the soy sauce and sweet white wine. Cover and simmer for 30 minutes. Next, add the coconut cream and the garlic and cook for a further 15 minutes. Remove from the heat, cover the pan with food wrap so it is airtight and infuse for 30 minutes.

Strain the stock obtained, pressing the mushrooms to release their full flavour (reserve the mushrooms). Return the stock to the boil, transfer to a processor, add the fresh herbs and process, adding the remaining 100 g of butter. Adjust the seasoning and strain through a fine chinois. The soup should be pale green and creamy. Keep warm (but do not boil any further).

2 FOR THE TOAST
Brown the mushrooms without oil in a non-stick frying pan. Transfer to a bowl and season with the mustard, Espelette pepper and salt. Leave to cool, then finely chop and spread on the slices of toast.

Finishing

Serve the soup with the warm toast. The Zézette soup can also be served with Gorgonzola gnocchi or with orzo.

True
SPRING

MENU
13

MAIN

Serves 6

2 shallots, chopped

50 g fresh butter

2 cloves garlic,
   green shoots removed, chopped

50 ml dry white wine

70 ml red port

300 g sausage meat
   from the butcher

150 g veal round, finely diced

100 g chicken livers, finely diced

15 g fresh herbs, chopped
   (parsley, chervil and chives)

1 egg

2 rounds puff pastry, 22 cm and 26 cm
   in diameter and 0.5 cm thick (ready-
   made)

1 egg yolk mixed with
   a little water, for brushing

100 g white mushrooms,
   browned in a pan and chopped

Salt and freshly ground black pepper

PREPARATION TIME | *35 minutes*   COOKING TIME | *40–50 minutes*

Meat Pithivier

Method

1 **FOR THE FILLING**
Brown the shallots in the fresh butter, then add the garlic, deglaze with the white wine and reduce until all of the liquid has evaporated. Add the port and leave to reduce by a further ¾ of its volume. Leave to cool completely.

Combine all meats, the shallots, herbs, egg and mushrooms. Adjust the seasoning and refrigerate for 2 hours.

2 **TO ASSEMBLE THE PITHIVIER**
Line a round pie tin with the 22-cm pastry. Place the filling in the centre. Brush all over with egg wash. Cover with the other pastry, pinching together the edges all around the circumference. Brush the top with egg and make a small depression in the middle, then use a knife to draw a decorative pattern. Leave to rest for 1 hour in the refrigerator. Preheat the oven to 200°C, 400°F, gas 6 and bake for 30 minutes, keeping an eye on the colour. Lower the oven temperature to 160°C, 325°F, gas 3 and bake for a further 10 minutes.

Finishing

Serve the Pithivier whole and cut it at the table, accompanied by a salad of baby spring greens or raw julienned vegetables.

True
SPRING

MENU
13

DESSERT

Serves 6

For the caramelised pears
4 Comice pears, peeled and roughly diced
150 g granulated sugar
Zest of 1 lemon
40 g butter

For the bavarois
100 g coconut milk
10 g granulated sugar
7 g gelatine, soaked in cold water for 1 hour
250 g coconut cream
2 drops bitter almond essence

For the tuiles
90 g muscovado sugar
30 g egg whites (1 white)
25 g melted butter
25 g flour

PREPARATION TIME | *35 minutes*   COOKING TIME | *15–20 minutes*

Caramelised pear brunoise
with coconut bavarois and muscovado tuiles

Method

1 FOR THE CARAMELISED PEARS
Combine the pears with the sugar and the lemon zest. Quickly sauté the pears in a non-stick frying pan with the butter until caramelised.

2 FOR THE BAVAROIS
Heat some of the coconut milk with the sugar. Remove from the heat, wring out the gelatine and add, along with the coconut cream and the remaining milk. Flavour with the bitter almond essence. Divide this bavarois between six deep dishes and refrigerate for 1 hour until set.

3 FOR THE TUILES
Combine the muscovado sugar with the egg white and leave to rest for 1 hour before adding the melted butter and the flour.
Preheat the oven to 180°C, 350°F, gas 4. Make circles of the mixture, 10 cm each in diameter, on a baking mat and bake for approximately 9 minutes. Remove the tuiles from the mat while still warm and set aside in a dry place.

Finishing

Once the dishes are fully chilled, place the still-warm caramelised pears on top of the bavarois. Finish with a muscovado tuile.

True
SPRING

MENU
14

STARTER

Serves 6

12 hard-boiled eggs,
    halved lengthways

2 tsp strong mustard

100 g crème fraîche

2 tbsp flat-leaf parsley, finely chopped

1 shallot, chopped

50 g butter

White balsamic vinegar

1 tbsp honey

Juice and zest of ½ lemon

60 ml olive oil

300 g mixture of baby salad leaves, herbs
    and edible flowers (pansies, nasturtium,
    etc.)

Salt and freshly ground black pepper

PREPARATION TIME | *25 minutes*

COOKING TIME | *16 minutes*

Eggs à la Berrichonne

Method

1 FOR THE EGGS
Gently remove the egg yolks and press through a sieve, then season with mustard and add the crème fraîche, parsley and shallot. Season with salt and pepper.
Fill the egg whites with this mixture. Heat the butter in a thick baking dish until melted and dark in colour. Place the egg halves face-up in the butter for 2–3 minutes. Deglaze with a spot of balsamic vinegar, turn over and leave face-down for a further 2–3 minutes.

2 FOR THE SALAD DRESSING
Dilute the honey with the lemon juice, then mix in the zest and oil using a whisk. Season with salt and drizzle over the salad leaves.

Finishing

Serve the eggs warm in their baking dish. The dressed salad should be served separately.

True
SPRING

MENU
14

MAIN

Serves 6

For the Sienna spices

4 tbsp white breadcrumbs

1 tbsp gingerbread, dried and crumbled into breadcrumbs

Skin of 1 orange, removed using a peeler

Skin of 1 lemon, removed using a peeler, flesh juiced

1 tsp mild curry powder

½ tsp paprika

½ tsp tandoori spice mix

200 g amaranth*

1 x 80 g slice smoked bacon, finely chopped and cooked

150 g baby spinach leaves, chopped

For the langoustines

24 large langoustine tails, peeled

Olive oil

60 g fresh butter

Dash lemon juice

2 limes, peeled and supremed

1 pack enokitake, roots removed and stalks separated from one another)**

Still mineral water

Salt

* (found in health food shops)
** (Japanese mushrooms, found in hypermarkets or Asian spice shops)

PREPARATION TIME | *20 minutes*      COOKING TIME | *10–15 minutes*

Sienna langoustines
with enokitake amaranth

Method

1 **FOR THE SIENNA SPICES** (make ahead)
Preheat the oven to 110°C, 225°F, gas ¼. Dry the citrus skins in the oven until they start to crack (allow 2–3 hours). Grind to a powder, then sieve. Combine the two types of breadcrumbs with the spices and the skins. Store in a dry place.

2 **FOR THE AMARANTH**
Cook the amaranth and the bacon in a pot of salted water for 10–15 minutes. Drain and immediately add to the spinach leaves. Combine and set aside, keeping warm.

3 **FOR THE LANGOUSTINES**
Season the langoustines lightly with salt and sauté in a very hot frying pan with a few drops of olive oil for 40 seconds. Next, add the Sienna spices and the butter, taking care to ensure that the butter does not brown. Deglaze with a dash of lemon juice. Drain the langoustines and pour the hot butter into the amaranth.

Finishing

Divide the amaranth between six large plates and add the langoustines and lime segments. Scatter the enokitake on top.

True
SPRING

MENU
14

DESSERT

Serves 6

For the mint syrup
125 g sugar
250 ml water
15 fresh mint leaves, whole
5 fresh mint leaves, chopped
2 tbsp mint liqueur

For the rocket chlorophyll
400 g fresh rocket,
   cleaned and ready for use
1.5 litres still mineral water

For the financiers
100 g whole eggs (2 small eggs or 1 ½
   medium)
100 g sugar
80 g butter, softened
100 g UHT cream
100 g ground white almonds
30 g flour

To serve
80 g fresh rocket, ready for use
Icing sugar
Vanilla ice cream

PREPARATION TIME | *30 minutes*

COOKING TIME | *22–25 minutes*

Financiers
with rocket chlorophyll and mint syrup

Method

1 FOR THE MINT SYRUP
Bring the water and sugar to a boil. Remove from the heat and add the whole mint leaves, then cover the pot with food wrap so it is airtight and infuse until completely cool. Strain, then add the chopped mint and the mint liqueur. Refrigerate.

2 FOR THE ROCKET CHLOROPHYLL
Process the rocket with the chilled water. Press through a cloth to extract as much as possible of the green liquid (the inside of the cloth should be completely dry). Heat the green juice obtained, stirring with a spatula until a green film forms on top. Carefully remove this film using a skimmer and place on a clean tea towel placed on a bed of crushed ice. Chlorophyll is a very deep green, with a highly potent taste.

3 FOR THE ROCKET FINANCIER
Preheat the oven to 130°C, 260°F, gas ½. Whisk the eggs and sugar together until the mixture turns pale. Add the butter. Combine 30 g of rocket chlorophyll with the cream and pour over the eggs, then combine until smooth. Combine the almond powder with the flour and add. Mix together. Transfer to financier baking tins (rectangular), or one of any shape, and bake for 12–15 minutes.

Finishing

Pour a bed of syrup into each of six deep dishes. Sprinkle some icing sugar over the rocket previously set aside for the garnish, then divide between the dishes, place the financiers on top and finish with a portion of vanilla ice cream.

True
SPRING

MENU
15

STARTER

Serves 6

For the Sauternes cubes
50 ml still mineral water
3 gelatine leaves,
    soaked in cold water
150 ml sweet Sauternes wine

For the green pea velouté
200 ml milk
350 g fresh peas, boiled in salted water
10 g fresh mint leaves
Fine salt and freshly ground white pepper

For the vegetables
6 baby carrots, boiled in salted water and
    cut into 2–3 pieces
6 mini leeks, boiled in salted water
    and cut into 2–3 pieces
6 mini turnips, boiled in salted water
    and cut into 2–3 pieces
6 white asparagus spears, boiled in salted
    water and cut into 2–3 pieces
6 baby onions, boiled in salted water
    and cut into 2–3 pieces
12 radishes, quartered
18 physalis fruits, halved

PREPARATION TIME | *30 minutes*

COOKING TIME | *5–15 minutes*

Green pea velouté
with Sauternes cubes and baby vegetables

Method

1 **FOR THE SAUTERNES CUBES**
Heat the water and dissolve the gelatine, then remove from the heat, add the Sauternes and stir in. Pour a layer 3 cm deep into a container and leave to set in the refrigerator, then cut into squares. Refrigerate again.

2 **FOR THE GREEN PEA VELOUTÉ**
Heat half of the milk and leave the mint to infuse, covered, until completely cool. Strain through a chinois, pressing the mint leaves. Process the peas in a blender, adding the remaining milk and the mint infusion to taste. Season with salt and pepper before straining through a fine chinois to produce a thick cream with a sauce-like consistency. Refrigerate.

Finishing

Distribute all of the vegetables and the physalis evenly between six deep dishes and add the Sauternes cubes. Spoon out a generous serving of chilled pea velouté to each guest at the table.
This dish can be served with edible flowers (pansies, sweet pea, nasturtium, etc.) or with other green vegetables (such as courgettes or green peppers).

True
SPRING

MENU
15

MAIN

Serves 6

For the Bellino stuffing

60 g pitted black olives in oil, chopped

60 g cured ham (equal quantities
of lean meat and fat), finely diced

2 anchovy fillets in oil, finely diced

40 g butter, softened
(left out at room temperature)

20 g white breadcrumbs

20 g ground white almonds

10 g mixture parsley and dill, chopped

20 ml white wine

10 ml lemon juice

20 ml garlic purée

For the fennel

3 bulbs fennel, halved

2 shallots, chopped

2 tomatoes, peeled and seeded

2 cloves garlic, crushed

1 sprig rosemary

Salt and freshly ground black pepper

For the red mullet

Olive oil

6 x 200 g red mullet,
filleted by the fishmonger

PREPARATION TIME | *25 minutes*

COOKING TIME | *1 hour 30 minutes approx.*

Red mullet with Bellino stuffing

Method

1 FOR THE BELLINO STUFFING
Combine the olives with the ham and anchovies. Add the softened butter, breadcrumbs and ground almonds. Mix well and add the chopped herbs, white wine, lemon juice and garlic.
Flatten the stuffing into a layer 5 mm thick between two sheets of food wrap. Chill to harden, then cut into 6 rectangles measuring 8 x 10 cm. Place each one on a sheet of baking paper.

2 FOR THE BRAISED CONFIT FENNEL
Boil the fennel bulbs for 10 minutes in salted water. Meanwhile, brown the shallots in a gratin dish. Add the tomatoes, garlic and rosemary, then season and leave to soften. Preheat the oven to 180°C, 350°F, gas 4. Drain the fennel bulbs and place on top of the tomato compote, then cover with aluminium foil and bake for 40–60 minutes: use the tip of a knife to check if they are ready.

3 TO COOK THE STUFFING AND RED MULLET
Place the Bellino stuffing rectangles on a baking sheet along with their paper and place under the grill to gratinate. Leave to cool at room temperature.
Sear the red mullet fillets skin-side down in a non-stick frying pan with a little olive oil for 3 minutes, then turn, reduce the heat and cook for a further 3–4 minutes.

Finishing

Divide the stuffing rectangles between 6 warmed plates and place the red mullet fillets on top. Serve the fennel bulbs in the centre of the table.

Serves 6

120 g lavender honey
50 ml white balsamic vinegar
350 g strawberries, hulled and chopped
250 g whole raspberries
250 g blackberries, halved
100 g redcurrants

PREPARATION TIME | *15 minutes*

COOKING TIME | *2 minutes*

Red berry salad
with melted lavender honey and white balsamic vinegar

Method

Gently heat the honey in a bain marie and thin by adding the vinegar. Leave to cool completely. Gently mix together the fruits with the honey to coat well.

Finishing

Serve the honeyed fruits in 6 dessert bowls. Can be served with a blackcurrant sorbet, lemon sablé biscuits or a pound cake.

Serves 6

1 very white whole cauliflower
    weighing 700–800 g, cleaned
8 g tandoori spice mix
2 g curry powder
3 g turmeric
8 g paprika
80 g white breadcrumbs
250 g fromage blanc

2 red onions, sliced into rings
20 ml sherry vinegar
20 ml olive oil
Coarse and fine salt
Sugar

PREPARATION TIME | *15 minutes*

COOKING TIME | *30–35 minutes*

Maharajah cauliflower

Method

1 FOR THE CAULIFLOWER
Cook the cauliflower whole in salted water for 20 minutes (tip: cover with a cloth to ensure even cooking). Drain, taking care that it does not fall apart. Leave to cool at room temperature.
In a bowl, combine the spices with the breadcrumbs, add the fromage blanc and mix to form a supple batter.

2 FOR THE ONIONS
Fry the onion rings in olive oil over a high heat. Add a little sugar and salt, then deglaze with the sherry vinegar and transfer while the onions are still crunchy. Leave to cool.

3 FOR THE SPICED CAULIFLOWER
Preheat the oven to 220°C, 425°F, gas 7. Place the cauliflower on a baking tray, coat completely in the spiced batter and bake for 6–8 minutes to gratinate.

Finishing

Serve the cauliflower whole at the table, carve and accompany with the sweet and sour onion rings and a slice of toasted country bread.

True
SPRING

MENU
16

MAIN

Serves 6

6 x 140 g skin-on sea bass steaks (filleted
by the fishmonger)

60 ml olive oil

Skin of ½ grapefruit

6 coriander seeds, crushed

1 soft cabbage (such as oxheart or pointed)

80 g fresh butter

Fine salt

Juice of ½ lime

120 g rocket, ready for use,
roughly chopped

12 semi-brined anchovy fillets,
finely and evenly diced

PREPARATION TIME | *20 minutes*

COOKING TIME | *20–30 minutes*

Grilled sea bass
with chopped rocket, semi-brined anchovy and cabbage

Method

1 **FOR THE MARINADE**
Combine the olive oil with the grapefruit skin and the coriander.
Marinate the sea bass steaks in this infused oil for approximately 2 hours.

2 **FOR THE BUTTERED CABBAGE**
Cut the cabbage into pieces, removing the large outer leaves. Leave
to soften in a casserole with the fresh butter. Season with salt.

3 **TO COOK THE SEA BASS**
Drain the fish and season with salt. Place the sea bass steaks skin-
side down in a frying pan and place under the grill for 3–4 minutes.
Set the oven to 200°C, 400°F, gas 6. Place the sea bass skin-side down
in a thick baking dish with the oil from the marinade and bake for 5–6
minutes. Check if cooking is complete by pressing with a fingertip.
Remove the steaks and dress with lime juice.

Finishing

Season the rocket with a little cooking juice, add the anchovies, then
divide between six deep dishes and place the cabbage and sea bass
steaks on top.

Serves 6

For the sweet pastry

100 g butter, softened
(left out at room temperature)

80 g icing sugar

Pinch of salt

200 g T55 flour

1 egg

For the rhubarb

500 g rhubarb, peeled, cleaned
and cut into 2 cm chunks

50 g white sugar

125 g double cream

60 g ground almonds

100 g brown sugar

2 eggs

50 g sliced almonds

Icing sugar

For the apricot coulis

250 ml still mineral water

125 g sugar

10 very ripe apricots, pitted
(or tinned cooked apricots in syrup)

PREPARATION TIME | *40 minutes*　　COOKING TIME | *1 hour 10 minutes*

Rhubarb tart
with apricot coulis

Method

1 **FOR THE SWEET PASTRY**
Make the sweet pastry base by following the instructions on p. 76, without cooking completely. Leave to cool.

2 **FOR THE RHUBARB**
Sweeten the chunks of rhubarb with white sugar, mix well and leave in a colander for around 2 hours to draw out the liquid. Combine the cream with the almond powder, brown sugar and eggs. Refrigerate.

3 **FOR THE APRICOT COULIS** (can be prepared well in advance)
Add a generous amount of sugar to the apricots and cook in a little water, covered, to a thick marmalade.

4 **TO BAKE THE TART**
Preheat the oven to 180°C, 350°F, gas 4. Cover the base of the pastry with the rhubarb and bake for 15 minutes. Add the almond and brown sugar cream and bake the tart for a further 15 minutes until golden. Spread out the sliced almonds on a baking sheet, sweeten with icing sugar and toast in the oven at 180°C, 350°F, gas 4 until brown (this can be done at the same time as the tart is baking).

Finishing

Sprinkle the caramelised sliced almonds over the still-warm tart, then place in the centre of the table to be sliced. Place the apricot coulis on each plate before adding the tart slices.

True
SPRING

MENU
17

STARTER

Serves 6

250 g daikon radish, finely diced

450 g lean beef (rump steak or tenderloin), diced

1 tsp chives, chopped

1 tsp parsley, chopped

1 shallot, chopped

1 tbsp capers, chopped

1 tbsp gherkins, chopped

2 raw egg yolks

200 g smoked eel, finely diced

Tabasco® sauce

Worcestershire sauce

Strong mustard

Olive oil

1 tsp black poppy seeds

Salt

PREPARATION TIME | *25 minutes*

COOKING TIME | *1 hour for the radish*

Steak and smoked eel tartare
with salted radish

Method

1 **FOR THE SALTED RADISH**
Place the radish in a colander, toss in 10 g salt and marinate for 1 hour at room temperature. Transfer to paper towels and leave to dry.

2 **FOR THE TARTARE**
Combine the beef with the herbs, shallot, capers and gherkins. Add the egg yolks. Add the eel and combine, taking care not to crush it, then season with salt, Tabasco®, Worcestershire sauce, mustard and olive oil. Keep this mixture chilled until serving.

Finishing

Gently transfer the tartare to moulds (there is no need to press or force it) before serving on plates. Combine the radish with the black poppy seeds and divide between the tartares.

Serves 6

6 x 100 g skinless croaker fish fillets

70 g butter

500 ml craft cider

90 g mange tout, trimmed
   and cut into matchsticks

1 tbsp olive oil

2 tbsp still mineral water

2 bunches watercress,
   leaves removed, ready for use

½ Camembert, (not too ripe), sliced

Salt and freshly ground black pepper

PREPARATION TIME | *25 minutes*

COOKING TIME | *20 minutes*

Croaker fish
in craft cider served with Camembert, watercress and mange tout

Method

1 **TO COOK THE FILLETS**
Heat the butter in a frying pan until bubbling. Season the croaker fish fillets and sear in the butter for 4 minutes on each side to stiffen. Remove the fish and keep warm. Deglaze the frying pan with the cider and leave to reduce by ¾. Finish cooking the fish in the reduced cider, for 7–8 minutes basting continuously with a spoon so that each piece is coated on all sides.

2 **FOR THE MANGE TOUT**
Heat the oil in a frying pan over a high heat, then very quickly sauté the mange tout. Season lightly with salt, deglaze with a little of the cooking cider from the fish and remove.

Finishing

Make a bed of watercress in the centre of each of 6 plates, then top with the slices of Camembert, the fish and the mange tout. Drizzle the remaining reduced cider over the whole dish. This dish can be served with basmati rice mixed with small cubes of mango and green apple.

True

SPRING

MENU
17

DESSERT

Serves 6

For the toasted flour sablé biscuits

180 g natural white T 55 flour

5 g baking powder

180 g butter, softened (left out at room temperature)

Pinch of salt

6 hard-boiled egg yolks, pressed through a sieve

45 g icing sugar

30 g ground almonds

For the chocolate Armagnac soufflé

Melted butter

40 g sugar + extra for the plate

Bitter cocoa powder

70 g egg yolks (2 yolks)

40 g still mineral water

100 ml Armagnac

60 g dark chocolate (70% cocoa), melted

120 g egg whites (3–4 whites), whisked into soft peaks

PREPARATION TIME | *20 minutes*

COOKING TIME | *40–42 minutes*

Chocolate Armagnac soufflé
with toasted flour sablé biscuits

Method

1 FOR THE TOASTED FLOUR (make ahead)
Spread out 135 g of the T 55 flour on a baking sheet, then bake at 160°C, 325°F, gas 3 for around 15 minutes, stirring often to produce a nice even golden colour.

2 FOR THE SABLÉ BISCUITS
Combine the toasted flour with the remaining 45 g flour and the baking powder. Add the salt, egg yolks, icing sugar and ground almonds to the butter and combine, then add the two flours. Leave to rest in the refrigerator for 30 minutes, then roll out to ½ cm thick and cut into 8 cm circles. Preheat the oven to 150°C, 300°F, gas 2 and bake for 20 minutes. Leave to cool before detaching them from the tray: they are too delicate when hot.

3 FOR THE CHOCOLATE ARMAGNAC SOUFFLÉ
Brush a large, deep dish with melted butter or a large porcelain dish (this will act as a baking dish), then sprinkle with sugar and cocoa. Preheat the oven to 200°C, 400°F, gas 6. Make a bain marie and warm the egg yolks, water, Armagnac and 20 g sugar, whisking. Once the mixture has reached a mousse-like texture, add the melted chocolate and mix well. Add the egg whites (without breaking their texture), then the 40 g of sugar. Transfer to the dish and bake for 10–12 minutes: the centre of the soufflé should still be runny.

Finishing

Serve the soufflé as is, dusted with cocoa powder and accompanied by the sablé biscuits.

True
SPRING

MENU
18

STARTER

Serves 6

50 g fresh butter

Juice of 1 lemon

100 ml still mineral water

600 g medium-sized white mushrooms,
cleaned and quartered

15 g strong Dijon mustard

60 g fromage frais

1 small tsp Colombo curry powder

500 ml olive oil

400 g small squid, cleaned
and sliced into rounds

150 ml intensely-flavoured olive oil

2 tbsp flat-leaf parsley, crushed

Fine salt and freshly ground white pepper

PREPARATION TIME | *30 minutes*

COOKING TIME | *15–20 minutes*

White mushrooms
in Colombo-style mustard sauce, served with squid rings

Method

1 **FOR THE MUSHROOMS**
Melt the butter in a saucepan with the lemon juice and mineral water. Season lightly with salt, then add the white mushrooms and stir. Bring to the boil (6 minutes approx.), then drain the mushrooms, reserving the liquid.
Reduce the cooking liquid by half, then remove from the heat and process along with the mustard, fromage frais and Colombo spices, gradually adding the olive oil. Pour this creamy stock over the mushrooms and return to the heat, but do not allow to boil.

2 **FOR THE SQUID**
Quickly fry the squid rings in intense olive oil, then season with salt and pepper.

Finishing

Serve the mushrooms in the saucepan at the table. Divide the squid between six deep dishes, previously warmed, and scatter with chopped flat-leaf parsley.

True
SPRING

MENU
18

MAIN

Serves 6

6 x 120 g skinless, boneless
 salmon steaks

For the marinade
100 g molasses
100 ml blonde beer
15 g wildflower honey
20 ml olive oil
30 ml nuoc-mâm
Pinch cayenne pepper

For the sorrel and raspberry fondue
200 g raspberries
20 g sugar
50 g fresh butter
250 g sorrel, cleaned and roughly chopped
Fine salt

Grilled salmon steak
flavoured with blonde beer, molasses and nuoc-mâm, served with sorrel and raspberry fondue

Method

1 FOR THE MARINADE
Thin the molasses by whisking in the beer, then add the remaining ingredients and mix well.

2 FOR THE SORREL AND RASPBERRY FONDUE
Cook the raspberries with the sugar for around 10 minutes. Meanwhile, melt the butter, add the sorrel, season and cook until all of its water has evaporated (around 10 minutes). Combine the sorrel with the raspberries, cook for a further 5 minutes and set aside, keeping warm.

3 FOR THE SALMON
Preheat the oven to 110°C, 225°F, gas ¼. Meanwhile, season the salmon steaks and grill on both sides. Place in a baking dish and cover in the molasses marinade. Bake for 10–15 minutes (press with a fingertip to check that they are cooked).

Finishing

Cover the bases of 6 plates with the sorrel and raspberry fondue. Cover with the salmon steaks, well coated in the marinade. This dish can be served with fried Ratte potatoes with golden sesame seeds and a raw fennel and ginger salad.

MENU
18

DESSERT

Serves 6

600 g very dark Burlat cherries, pitted
120 g brown sugar
Juice of ½ lemon
2–4 Haribo Zan® cubes
(anise flavour; to taste)

For the Amaretto syrup

300 g very dark Burlat cherries, pitted
30 ml Amaretto (almond liqueur)
Vanilla or licorice ice cream

PREPARATION TIME | *30 minutes*

COOKING TIME | *15 minutes*

Pan-fried Burlat cherries in brown sugar
and Zan®, served with Amaretto cherry syrup

Method

1 **FOR THE PAN-FRIED CHERRIES**
Place the pitted cherries, brown sugar, lemon juice and Zan® cubes in a hot non-stick frying pan. Cook for 10–15 minutes, stirring constantly, until the cherries release some of their liquid and combine with the sugar and Zan® to form a thick syrup to coat the fruit. Transfer to a large bowl and leave to cool at room temperature.

2 **FOR THE AMARETTO SYRUP**
Process the cherries in a blender, then strain and add the Amaretto. Let stand in the refrigerator.

Finishing

Divide the chilled pan-fried cherries, fully coated in their cooking syrup, between six dessert bowls and top with the ice cream of your choice. Serve the chilled Amaretto jus in six small glasses to be drunk alongside the dessert.

MENUS

SUMMER

July | *August*

SUMMER

MENU
19

| STARTER | MAIN | DESSERT |

Stuffed tomatoes with aubergine caviar
and fresh Picodon cheese

Sweet and sour rabbit fricassee
with nougatine shards
and baby carrots

Peach quarters with verbena,
green almonds
and almond cake

SUMMER

MENU
20

| STARTER | MAIN | DESSERT |

Cured ham, fresh figs
and grilled prawns with pink peppercorns

"Elephant ears"
with girolle mushrooms and spring onions

Stuffed Bergeron apricots with frangipane
and pistachio cream

SUMMER

MENU
21

| STARTER | MAIN | DESSERT |

Burgundy snails with watercress,
crisp brick pastry and bacon

Poached ray cooked in brown butter,
served with chard stalk Grenobloise

Chocolate-topped biscuits
with raspberry purée

SUMMER

MENU

22

| *page 152* |

| STARTER | MAIN | DESSERT |

Flat omelette with tarragon,
horns of plenty
and green beans

Roast saddle of lamb with savory,
served with aubergine confit

Watermelon, melon, cucumber and
redcurrant salad with Campari®

SUMMER

MENU

23

| *page 158* |

| STARTER | MAIN | DESSERT |

Cream of rice with sweet garlic,
cherry tomatoes and poached langoustines

Devilled chicken
and semi-dried melon with black pepper

Intense olive oil ice cream
with candied fruit, pine nuts
and green Verveine du Velay sheep's yoghurt

SUMMER

MENU

24

| *page 164* |

| STARTER | MAIN | DESSERT |

Pan-fried cherry tomatoes
with cuttlefish, smoked duck and basil

Whiting fillets with lemon jelly
and rocket and parsley mashed potatoes

Vanilla Swiss roll
with strawberry juice

MENU
19

STARTER

Serves 6

For the aubergine caviar

2 whole aubergines (very firm and not too large), halved lengthways

120 ml olive oil

2 sprigs fresh thyme

2 bay leaves

3 cloves garlic, unpeeled and bruised

1 shallot, chopped

3 x 45–60 g Picodon goat's cheese, diced

1 tbsp chives, chopped

6 x 140 g tomatoes (choose nice-looking ones)

½ tsp sugar

20 ml white balsamic vinegar

100 g ready-to-use baby spinach leaves, chopped

Fine salt and white pepper

PREPARATION TIME | *20 minutes*

COOKING TIME | *35–40 minutes*

Stuffed tomatoes
with aubergine caviar and fresh Picodon cheese

Method

1 FOR THE AUBERGINE CAVIAR
Preheat the oven to 180°C, 350°F, gas 4. Make slits in the aubergine flesh, sprinkle with salt and leave on paper towels for 30 minutes to draw out the liquid. Dry well before browning in a frying pan with 60 ml olive oil. Transfer to a baking dish and season with the thyme, bay leaves, garlic and pepper. Cover with aluminium foil and bake for around 30 minutes.

Leave to cool, then use a spoon to separate the skins from the flesh. Chop the flesh, then fry in a dry pan with the shallot to dry out (the vegetable juices should evaporate). Leave to cool completely, then add the Picodon and the chives.

2 FOR THE TOMATOES
Remove the stems from the tomatoes, then cut off the tops. Carefully scoop out the flesh with a teaspoon, reserving the insides. Sprinkle some salt and sugar inside the tomatoes, then turn upside-down and leave for 25–30 minutes to draw out the liquid. Preheat the oven to 180°C, 350°F, gas 4. Place the tomatoes upside-down on a baking dish filled with rice. Bake for 5–7 minutes. Turn over and leave to cool, then fill each tomato with the aubergine–Picodon caviar. Replace the tops.

3 FOR THE TOMATO JUICE
Season the tomato flesh with salt and pepper, then process, adding the balsamic vinegar and the remaining olive oil. Strain through a chinois.

Finishing

Dress the baby spinach leaves with a little of the tomato juice and divide between 6 deep dishes. Place a stuffed tomato on each dish, then serve the remaining tomato juice in a separate bowl or glass.

MENU
19

MAIN

Serves 6

6 rabbit thighs (ask the butcher to remove the bones)

2 onions, finely diced

200 g butter

3 tbsp brown sugar

1 red pepper, peeled and finely diced

20 ml sherry vinegar

30 ml red balsamic vinegar

100 ml white wine

2 tomatoes, peeled, seeded and finely diced

80 g flour

30 baby carrots, peeled and ready for use

½ tsp white sugar

½ tsp cumin seed

Still mineral water

120 g nougatine, broken into rough shards (from a specialist bakery)

Fine salt and Espelette pepper

PREPARATION TIME | *30 minutes*

COOKING TIME | *30–35 minutes*

Sweet and sour rabbit fricassée
with nougatine shards and baby carrots

Method

1 FOR THE RABBIT
Sweat the onions in 20 g butter until golden. Add the brown sugar and caramelise. Add the red pepper, cook for 3–4 minutes, then add the two vinegars and the white wine. Bring to the boil, then add the tomatoes and leave to soften over a low heat.

Meanwhile, cut the rabbit thighs into small chunks. Season with salt and Espelette pepper, then coat in flour, tapping to remove any excess. Brown in a frying pan with 80 g butter, then add the rabbit to the sweet and sour compote and leave to simmer gently, covered, for 25–30 minutes.

2 FOR THE CARROTS
Spread out the carrots in a large, shallow saucepan, then add the white sugar, cumin, and 100 g of the cubed butter. Add mineral water until fully submerged, then cover with baking paper and cook over a medium heat. When finished, the water should have evaporated and the carrots should be very shiny and slightly crunchy.

Finishing

Serve the rabbit very hot in its pan, scattered with a few shards of nougatine. Serve the carrots in a separate dish or on the plates.

MENU
19

DESERT

Serves 6

You will need a circular cake tin 23 cm in diameter

4–6 peaches (depending on the size), peeled, pitted and quartered

500 ml still mineral water

250 g sugar

10 g verbena leaves

For the almond cake

3 eggs

115 g granulated sugar + 15 g for the meringue

1 tbsp amaretto

90 g potato starch

115 g ground almonds

90 g melted butter

60 g fresh almonds, shelled and peeled

Icing sugar

PREPARATION TIME | *20 minutes*

COOKING TIME | *10 minutes*

Peach quarters with verbena,
green almonds and almond cake

Method

1 FOR THE PEACH QUARTERS
Bring the water to the boil with the sugar, then add the verbena. Pour the boiling mixture over the peaches, then cover with food wrap, making sure it is airtight, and infuse until completely cool (if using white peaches, lemon juice must be added before adding the syrup).

2 FOR THE ALMOND CAKE
Preheat the oven to 170°C, 340°F, gas 3 ½. Beat 2 eggs and 1 egg yolk with the sugar until the mixture turns pale. Add the amaretto and use a spatula to stir in the starch and the almond powder, followed by the butter.
Whip the remaining egg white into soft peaks, then add the 15 g sugar to make a meringue. Carefully fold the meringue into the amaretto mixture. Transfer to a cake tin and bake for approximately 9 minutes, using the tip of a knife to check if they are ready.

Finishing

Serve the peach quarters with the syrup in individual dessert bowls. Scatter with fresh almonds. Serve the almond cake on a platter, dust with icing sugar and cut at the table. This dessert can be served with peach sorbet or fromage blanc ice cream.

MENU
20

STARTER

Serves 6

18 medium-sized prawns, peeled

30 ml olive oil

½ tsp pink peppercorns, crushed

Zest and juice of ½ lime

5 g fresh ginger, grated

6 very thin slices cured ham

9 fresh figs, quartered

1 tsp chives, chopped

Salt

PREPARATION TIME | *15 minutes*   **COOKING TIME** | *10 minutes*

Cured ham, fresh figs
and grilled prawns with pink peppercorns

Method

1 **FOR THE PRAWNS**
Season the prawns and place under the grill in a very hot non-stick frying pan with the olive oil and pink peppercorns. Remove and set aside the prawns and the cooking fat, leaving the pink peppercorns in the pan. Add the lime zest and ginger and set aside at room temperature.

2 **FOR THE HAM**
Cut the cured ham into wide but extremely thin slices.

Finishing

Divide the fig quarters between six plates. Just before serving, add the lime juice, ginger and chives to the prawns and combine. Add to the plates, then drizzle with the pink peppercorn and lemon zest juice. Top with a little mound of cured ham.

SUMMER

MENU
20

MAIN

Serves 6

6 x 150 g veal escalopes (flattened by the butcher)

2 eggs

1 tbsp olive oil

150 g flour

300 g white breadcrumbs

150 g butter

30 ml sunflower oil

12 medium spring onions
(leave the white bulbs whole, but chop the nicest green leaves)

800 g cleaned girolle mushrooms

Fine salt and freshly ground white pepper

PREPARATION TIME | *30 minutes*

COOKING TIME | *15–20 minutes*

"Elephant ears"
with girolle mushrooms and spring onions

Method

1 **FOR THE BREADED ESCALOPE "EARS"**
Beat the eggs together with the oil and season with salt and pepper. Set out a bowl with the flour, another with the egg and another for the breadcrumbs. Dip the escalopes first in the flour, then in the egg, then in the breadcrumbs. Fry in a pan with 30 g brown butter and a little sunflower oil.

2 **FOR THE MUSHROOMS AND ONIONS**
Boil the white onion bulbs in salted water, then drain on a tea towel. Leave to cool, then halve the bulbs. Brown the flat side of the onion bulbs in a frying pan with 30 g butter.
Meanwhile, gently sweat the green part of the onions with another 40 g butter.
Sauté the girolle mushrooms in a frying pan with the remaining butter. Once cooked, season with salt, add the green onion and keep warm.

Finishing

Serve the escalopes and roasted onion bulbs on flat plates, with the mushrooms on a separate platter.

Serves 6

12 apricots, halved
and pitted

For the frangipane

100 g butter, softened

100 g granulated sugar

100 g ground almonds

50 g chopped pistachios

2 eggs

For the pistachio cream

4 egg yolks

125 g sugar

500 ml milk

40 g pistachios, processed into a purée,
    or ready-made pistachio paste

50 ml water

20 g sugar

50 g butter

PREPARATION TIME | *20 minutes*

COOKING TIME | *25–30 minutes*

Stuffed Bergeron apricots
with frangipane and pistachio cream

Method

1 **FOR THE FRANGIPANE**
Combine the butter and sugar with a spatula until the mixture turns pale. Add the ground almonds and the chopped pistachios, then add the eggs one by one. Let stand for around 20 minutes at room temperature.

2 **FOR THE PISTACHIO CREAM**
Beat together the egg yolks and sugar until the mixture turns pale. Boil the milk, then pour over the eggs little by little, whisking. Return to a low heat, stirring constantly, until the cream is thick enough to coat the spatula (but without ever allowing to boil). Transfer to a large bowl, add the pistachio paste, process and chill in the refrigerator.

3 **TO COOK THE APRICOTS**
Preheat the oven to 180°C, 350°F, gas 4. Using a piping bag, line the inside of the apricots with the frangipane. Place the water, sugar and diced butter in a baking dish, add the stuffed apricots and bake for 15–20 minutes.
The frangipane should turn amber in colour, while the apricots should hold their shape and the liquid should reduce to almost nothing. Leave to cool at room temperature.

Finishing

Serve the apricots warm in their baking dish. Serve the chilled pistachio cream separately in a sauce boat.

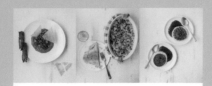

SUMMER

MENU
21

STARTER

Serves 6

4 dozen cooked Burgundy snails
  in court-bouillon

3 sheets brick pastry

120 g butter

12 very fine slices bacon

2 bunches watercress leaves, removed
  from stalks

250 ml milk

2 cloves garlic, crushed to a paste

1 tomato, peeled, seeded
  and chopped

1 shallot, chopped

Coarse and fine salt and freshly ground
  white pepper

PREPARATION TIME | *20 minutes*   COOKING TIME | *30–40 minutes*

Burgundy snails
with watercress, crisp brick pastry and bacon

Method

1 FOR THE BRICK PASTRY
Preheat the oven to 180°C, 350°F, gas 4. Brush the brick pastry sheets with 10 g melted butter. Cut out 18 triangles, place on a baking sheet and brown in the oven for 5–7 minutes.

2 FOR THE BACON
Place the bacon between two sheets of baking paper and sandwich these between two baking sheets. Bake in the oven at 180°C, 350°F, gas 4 until crisp and golden (10–20 minutes).

3 FOR THE WATERCRESS VELOUTÉ
Chop 2 tbsp of the watercress and set aside. Boil the rest of the watercress in salted water, then cool in cold water, drain and squeeze to remove as much of the water as possible. Heat 60 g butter until brown, then halt the cooking process by adding the cold milk. Process the watercress in a blender with the milk and butter mixture, then season (you should be left with a creamy, green sauce).

4 FOR THE SNAILS
Drain the snails well and fry with the remaining butter and the garlic, tomato and shallot. Add the chopped watercress at the end and adjust the seasoning to taste.

Finishing

Pour a layer of hot watercress velouté into each of 6 deep dishes. Divide the snails between the dishes, then top with the sheets of brick pastry and the bacon, crumbled if desired.

Serves 6

For the ray

6 x 250–300 g ray wings (scrubbed under running water to remove the slime)

400 g carrots, finely sliced

400 g onions, chopped

1 lemon, sliced

1 bouquet garni

1 tsp crushed white pepper

400 ml dry white wine

200 ml white wine vinegar

3 litres still mineral water

Coarse salt

120 g butter

1 freshly-squeezed lemon

For the chard stalk Grenobloise

500 g chard stalks, cut into small chunks

200 g chard leaves, very finely chopped

60 g butter

200 g double cream

2 tbsp capers

1 tbsp gherkins, chopped

For the croutons

2 slices sandwich bread, diced

40 ml sunflower oil

To finish

30 g capers, chopped

2 limes, supremed and diced

1 tbsp chives, chopped

Fine salt and freshly ground white pepper

PREPARATION TIME | *40 minutes*

COOKING TIME | *1 hour*

Poached ray
cooked in brown butter, served with chard stalk Grenobloise

Method

1 TO POACH THE RAY IN COURT-BOUILLON
Combine the vegetables with the lemon, bouquet garni and pepper in a large saucepan. Add the white wine, vinegar and water, season with coarse salt, then bring to the boil and simmer for 15–20 minutes. Strain the court-bouillon obtained.
Place the ray in a deep dish, pour the court-bouillon on top and poach the ray in the simmering liquid for 12–15 minutes. Drain, carefully remove the two fish skins while still hot.

2 FOR THE CHARD STALK GRENOBLOISE
Boil the white chard stalks in salted water, then halt the cooking process by adding chilled water.
Preheat the oven to 180°C, 350°F, gas 4. Sweat the chard leaves in a large saucepan with the butter, then add the drained stalks, the capers, gherkins and chives. Pour in the cream, bring to the boil and adjust the seasoning to taste. Transfer to a gratin dish and bake for 15 minutes.

3 FOR THE CROUTONS
While the chard is baking, brown the bread in a frying pan with the sunflower oil, then drain on paper towels.

Finishing

Fry the ray wings in brown butter and lemon juice just before serving onto plates. Scatter the capers, diced lime, chives and croutons over the chard and serve hot.

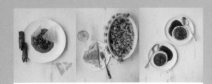

Serves 6

For the Succès biscuits
70 g ground almonds
70 g icing sugar
125 g egg whites
125 g sugar
Butter, for greasing

For the ganache
350 g double cream
150 g dark chocolate, broken up

For the raspberry purée
225 g raspberries
100 g sugar
1 gelatine leaf,
    soaked in cold water
Juice of ½ lemon

PREPARATION TIME | *1 hour*   COOKING TIME | *1 hour*

Chocolate-topped biscuits
with raspberry purée

Method

1 **FOR THE SUCCÈS BISCUITS**
Preheat the oven to 180°C, 350°F, gas 4. Combine the ground almonds with the icing sugar. Whip the egg whites into firm peaks, then add the sugar to produce a smooth meringue. Gently fold the two mixtures together. Transfer to a piping bag fitted with a smooth nozzle, then pipe 6 spirals, each 10 cm in diameter, on a lightly greased baking sheet. Bake for 10 minutes, then lower the temperature to 160°C, 325°F, gas 3 and bake for a further 30 minutes.

2 **FOR THE WHIPPED GANACHE**
Boil 150 g of the cream, then pour over the chocolate, stirring with a spatula until melted. Leave to cool.
Boil the remaining cream and pour over the ganache, mix well and let stand in the refrigerator. Next, use a whisk to whip the ganache until it turns pale and its texture is light and smooth. Transfer to a piping bag fitted with a wide, fluted nozzle.

3 **FOR THE RASPBERRY PURÉE**
Cook the raspberries with the sugar over a medium heat for around 10 minutes, then wring out the gelatine leaf and add, along with the lemon juice. Cook for a further 5 minutes before setting aside to cool.

Finishing

Pipe the ganache onto the biscuit bases. Divide the raspberry purée between six deep dishes and place the chocolate-covered biscuits on top. You can also add a few whole raspberries, chocolate shavings or even some chopped mint leaves.

MENU
22

STARTER

Serves 6

200 g horn of plenty mushrooms
80 g butter
1 shallot, chopped
12 eggs
1 tbsp fresh tarragon, chopped
400 g green beans
2 small spring onions, chopped
20 ml olive oil
1 tbsp white balsamic vinegar
Fine salt and paprika

PREPARATION TIME | *30 minutes*

COOKING TIME | *20–30 minutes*

Flat omelette with tarragon,
horns of plenty and green beans

Method

1 FOR THE HORNS OF PLENTY
Fry the horns of plenty with 20 g butter and the shallot. Season, leave to cool and roughly chop.

2 FOR THE OMELETTE
Beat the eggs in a large bowl with the tarragon, taking care not to over-beat, then season with the salt and paprika. The easiest thing is to make three small omelettes. Heat 20 g butter in a non-stick pan until golden, then pour in ⅓ of the egg, stirring with a fork. Stop stirring and leave the omelette to brown. Flip the omelette (place a plate upside-down on top of the pan, turn over and then slide the omelette from the plate back to the pan), then cook for a further 2 minutes and remove (lift out of the pan). Repeat this process for the remaining two omelettes.

3 FOR THE GREEN BEANS
Boil the green beans in salted water. Drain, then combine with the spring onions and season with salt, paprika, olive oil and balsamic vinegar.

Finishing

Serve the omelettes on plates and top with the still-warm horns of plenty. The green beans should be served in a bowl in the centre of the table.

SUMMER

MENU

22

MAIN

Serves 6

24 thick round aubergine slices (2.5–3 cm), skin still attached (4–5 aubergines)

300 ml olive oil

1 onion, diced

1 tomato, peeled, seeded and diced

70 g wildflower honey

70 ml sherry vinegar

5 cloves garlic, peeled and crushed

Espelette pepper

Fine salt

1 x 2.5–2.8 kg lamb saddle, prepared by the butcher

50 ml olive oil

1 bunch savory, chopped (if unavailable, substitute thyme; set aside a small amount to serve)

3 cloves garlic, unpeeled and bruised

2 shallots, quartered

Fine salt and pepper

PREPARATION TIME | *40 minutes*   COOKING TIME | *45–50 minutes*

Roast saddle of lamb
with savory, served with aubergine confit

Method

1 **FOR THE AUBERGINES** (Prepare one day in advance if possible, or the morning of the dinner)

Make slits in both sides of the aubergine slices to form a grid pattern, without cutting the skin. Salt both sides, then leave for around 20 minutes on paper towels to draw out the liquid.

Preheat the oven to 150°C, 300°F, gas 2. Bake the aubergines for 15 minutes in a casserole dish with 150 ml of the olive oil, and the onion, tomato, honey, vinegar, garlic and Espelette pepper.

Pat the aubergine slices dry, then brown in a frying pan with the remaining oil. Arrange on a plate and pour over the hot oil with the onion, tomato, honey, garlic and herbs. Bake, covered, for around 10 minutes (use the tip of a knife to check if the aubergines are cooked). Leave to cool in the baking dish.

2 **FOR THE LAMB SADDLE**

Preheat the oven to 200°C, 400°F, gas 6. Heat the olive oil in a roasting tin, season the lamb saddle and brown in the pan, beginning with the fattiest part. Roast in the oven for 10 minutes. Add the savory, garlic and shallots, then cook for a further 30 minutes or so, turning and basting the meat regularly. Remove the saddle, wrap in aluminium foil and leave to stand for 15–20 minutes.

Remove ¾ of the fatty juices from the roasting tin using a spoon, then deglaze with 60 ml of water and strain the fatty juices from the meat.

Finishing

Serve the aubergine confit in their baking dish in the centre of the table. Present the saddle whole in a warmed dish with a little fresh savory to intensify the flavour and serve the hot juices in a sauce boat. This dish can be accompanied by fried baby Ratte potatoes, also seasoned with savory and garlic.

SUMMER

MENU
22

DESSERT

Serves 6

250 ml still mineral water

125 g sugar

Peel of 3 lemons,
  removed using a peeler

2 gelatine leaves,
  soaked in cold water

Juice of ½ lemon

300 g watermelon, seeds removed

300 g melon, peeled and seeds removed

120 g cucumber, peeled and seeds removed

60 g redcurrants, removed from the vine

20 ml Campari®

Watermelon, melon,
cucumber and redcurrant salad with Campari®

Method

1 **FOR THE SYRUP**
Heat the mineral water with the sugar and lemon peel. Once the sugar has dissolved, wring out the gelatine and add, stirring in with a whisk to dissolve, then add the lemon juice. Strain and leave to cool at room temperature.

2 **FOR THE CAMPARI® FRUIT SALAD**
Cut the melon and watermelon into even-sized cubes. Cut the cucumber into smaller cubes (the same size as the redcurrants). In a mixing bowl, combine all of the fruits and the cucumber. Pour the Campari® into the syrup and drizzle over the fruit salad. Chill in the refrigerator.

Finishing

Serve the Campari® fruit salad in individual dessert bowls.
This dessert can be accompanied by a raspberry sorbet or French macarons.

MENU
23

STARTER

Serves 6

For the cream of rice

300 ml still mineral water

200 ml milk

50 g white rice

50 g pink garlic, peeled and green germ removed

100 g double cream

12 cherry tomatoes, quartered

1 shallot, chopped

1 tbsp chopped mixed herbs (parsley, chives, chervil, etc.)

40 ml olive oil

20 ml white balsamic vinegar

Fine salt and Espelette pepper

18 langoustine tails

Juice of 1 lemon

PREPARATION TIME | *30 minutes*   COOKING TIME | *25–30 minutes*

Cream of rice with sweet garlic,
cherry tomatoes and poached langoustines

Method

1 **FOR THE CREAM OF RICE**
Place the water and milk in a saucepan, season lightly with salt and bring to the boil. Add the rice and garlic, cover and cook for 20 minutes. Process in a blender, adding the cream.

2 **FOR THE TOMATOES**
Combine the tomatoes with the shallot and the herbs, then season with olive oil, vinegar, salt and Espelette pepper.

3 **FOR THE LANGOUSTINES** (to be poached just before serving)
Fill a saucepan with two glasses of water, a little salt and the lemon juice. Bring to a simmer and immerse the langoustines for 4–5 minutes, then drain.

Finishing

Divide the warm cream of rice between six deep dishes, then place the seasoned tomatoes on top and finish with the hot langoustine tails.

MENU
23

MAIN

Serves 6

For the melon

1 melon, peeled, seeds removed,
   cut into 2 cm slices

Icing sugar

1 tbsp crushed black peppercorns

Fine salt

For the devilled sauce

2 shallots, chopped

80 ml dry white wine

40 ml sherry vinegar

½ tsp black peppercorns, crushed

1 tomato, roughly chopped

500 ml brown chicken or beef
   stock (ready-made)

To sauté the chicken

8 skinless chicken breasts, diced

120 g butter

20 ml sunflower oil

300 g white mushrooms,
   cut into small segments

1 red pepper, peeled
   and finely diced

1 yellow pepper, peeled
   and finely diced

1 tsp chervil, crushed

1 tsp tarragon, chopped

 PREPARATION TIME | *40 minutes*

 COOKING TIME | *35 minutes*

Devilled chicken
and semi-dried melon with black pepper

Method

1 **FOR THE SEMI-DRIED MELON WITH PEPPER** (can be prepared a day in advance)

Preheat the oven to 110°C, 225°F, gas ¼. Sprinkle each slice of melon with icing sugar and season with salt and pepper. Spread out onto a non-stick baking sheet and bake for at least 2 hours, turning regularly, until dehydrated and half-candied. Leave to cool at room temperature, then refrigerate without allowing the slices to overlap.

2 **FOR THE DEVILLED SAUCE**

Place the shallots, white wine, vinegar and pepper in a saucepan. Reduce until almost dry, then add the tomato and continue cooking until soft. Add the brown stock, bring to the boil and simmer for around 10 minutes, then strain this devilled sauce through a chinois.

3 **FOR THE SAUTÉED CHICKEN**

Season the chicken pieces with salt, then fry with 50 g of the butter and the sunflower oil. Sauté the mushrooms in 50 g butter and season with salt once golden. Sweat the diced pepper in the remaining butter, then add the chicken, mushrooms and devilled sauce. Bring to the boil, adjust the seasoning to taste and simmer for around 15 minutes. Add the chopped herbs before serving.

Finishing

Serve the devilled chicken pieces in an attractive pot; the melon slices can be served directly on the plates. This dish can be accompanied by potato matchsticks, paprika-flavoured crisps or slightly crunchy gourmet green beans.

Serves 6

For the olive oil ice cream

120 ml still mineral water

70 ml lemon juice

Grated zest of ½ unwaxed lemon

150 g granulated sugar

120 g crème fraîche

250 g intense olive oil
(with strong flavour)

90 g egg whites (3 whites)

For the Verveine du Velay yoghurt

80 g brown sugar

1 sheep's yoghurt (150 g approx.)

30–50 ml green Verveine du Velay
(herb liqueur, to taste)

60 g sweet whipped cream

For the candied fruit and pine nuts

240 g diced candied fruit mix

60 g pine nuts, toasted in the oven and
crushed

PREPARATION TIME | *20 minutes*   **FREEZING TIME** | *2–3 hours*

Intense olive oil ice cream
with candied fruit, pine nuts and
green Verveine du Velay sheep's yoghurt

Method

1 FOR THE OLIVE OIL ICE CREAM
Bring the water to a boil with the sugar and the lemon juice and zest. Leave to cool. Combine the cooled syrup with the crème fraîche and olive oil. Whip the egg whites into soft peaks and gently fold in to the olive oil cream using a spatula. Transfer to an ice-cream maker and freeze for 2–3 hours.

2 FOR THE GREEN VERVEINE DU VELAY SHEEP'S YOGHURT
Combine the sugar, yoghurt and Verveine du Velay, then add the whipped cream and refrigerate.

3 FOR THE CANDIED FRUIT AND PINE NUTS
Form the candied fruits into 6 fairly tall discs, then roll in the crushed pine nuts.

Finishing

Divide the yoghurt between 6 bowls or deep dishes, then place the candied fruit discs in the centre of each and top with a generous scoop of olive ice cream. This dessert can be served with a nice orange or almond tuile, or a few soft ladyfingers.

Serves 6

30 cherry tomatoes

150 g cuttlefish, ready for use

40 ml olive oil

20 ml maple syrup

20 ml sherry vinegar

½ smoked duck magret, wiped to remove
    some of the fat and diced

1 tbsp basil, chopped

Fine salt and freshly ground black pepper

PREPARATION TIME | *15 minutes*

COOKING TIME | *40 minutes*

Pan-fried cherry tomatoes
with cuttlefish, smoked duck and basil

Method

1 FOR THE CUTTLEFISH
Season the cuttlefish, grease with 10 ml of the olive oil and sear quickly in a very hot, dry non-stick frying pan. Leave to cool and finely dice.

2 FOR THE TOMATOES
Heat the remaining olive oil in a frying pan, then add the tomatoes, season with salt and leave to cook, uncovered, over a low heat for around 20 minutes to soften. Add the maple syrup and the vinegar: the tomatoes should burst and soften. Stir often with a wooden spoon and baste regularly.

3 TO COOK THE DUCK BREAST
Quickly sauté the diced duck breast in a dry frying pan, then drain once cooked.

4 TO PAN FRY THE TOMATOES, DUCK AND CUTTLEFISH
Combine the three ingredients in a frying pan and cook together for ten minutes or so. Add quite a lot of pepper at the last moment.

Finishing

This starter can be served as is on a platter, or in individual ramekins, accompanied by a green bean salad.

SUMMER

MENU
24

MAIN

Serves 6

6 whitings, filleted and boned
  by the fishmonger (reserve the skin)

For the lemon jelly

100 ml freshly-squeezed lemon juice,
  strained

100 ml water

40 g sugar

2 g agar agar

2 gelatine leaves,
  soaked in cold water

Zest of ¼ unwaxed lemon

For the mash

1 kg potatoes, peeled and diced

80 g butter

180 ml milk

180 ml double cream

2 tbsp flat-leaf parsley, chopped

60 g rocket, roughly chopped

For the whiting

3 eggs, beaten

2 tbsp sunflower oil

160 g flour

300 g white breadcrumbs

1 litre olive oil

Fine salt

PREPARATION TIME | *30 minutes*

COOKING TIME | *15 minutes*

Whiting fillets
with lemon jelly and rocket and parsley mashed potatoes

Method

1 FOR THE LEMON JELLY
If possible, prepare 4–5 hours in advance. Combine the lemon juice, water, sugar and agar agar. Bring to the boil, stirring with a whisk. Remove from the heat and dissolve the gelatine in the hot liquid, then add the lemon zest. Transfer to a large bowl and leave to set in the refrigerator. Process the firm mass to a smooth, creamy jelly.

2 FOR THE MASHED POTATOES
Boil the potatoes in salted water, drain, cool under cold water and press through a fine sieve using a spatula. Meanwhile, bring the milk and cream to a boil. Transfer the potatoes to a saucepan, stir in the butter using a spatula and thin with the hot milk and cream. Add the parsley and rocket, and adjust the seasoning to taste.

3 FOR THE WHITING
Beat the eggs together with the sunflower oil, then season. Coat the whiting fillets first in the egg, then the flour and finally the breadcrumbs. Heat the olive oil to approximately 170°C, 340°F, gas 3½ in a large, oval frying pan. Fry the fillets for 5–6 minutes. Drain on paper towels, then season with salt.

Finishing

Arrange the whiting fillets on large flat plates and accompany with a spoonful of mashed potato. Serve the lemon jelly as a condiment in a separate ramekin for each guest, and the remaining mash in a dish at the table.

Serves 6

For the sponge
3 eggs + 3 yolks
80 g sugar
80 g flour
20 g butter, melted with the seeds
    of one vanilla pod

For the pastry cream
3 egg yolks
70 g sugar
55 g flour
350 ml milk
1 vanilla pod, halved

For the strawberry juice
200 g strawberries, cleaned and hulled
80 g sugar
100 ml milk
Juice of ½ lemon

PREPARATION TIME | *25 minutes*

COOKING TIME | *25 minutes*

Vanilla Swiss roll
with strawberry juice

Method

1 FOR THE SPONGE
Preheat the oven to 180°C, 350°F, gas 4. Combine the whole eggs with the yolks and the sugar. Place in a simmering bain marie and beat until thick and mousse-like. Remove from the heat and continue beating to bring the temperature down. Combine the flour with the whisked yolks. Mix a little of this batter into the vanilla-scented butter, then fold in the rest with a spatula. Spread out the batter over a non-stick Swiss roll tin and bake for 10 minutes. Remove from the oven and transfer to a cooling rack.

2 FOR THE PASTRY CREAM
Whisk together the egg yolks and sugar until the mixture turns pale, then add the flour and mix to combine. Bring the milk to the boil with the vanilla, then pour over the yolks, stirring. Return the mixture to the pan and thicken over a low heat, whisking (5–6 minutes). Transfer to another container, remove the vanilla pod, cover the surface of the cream with food wrap and chill.

3 TO ASSEMBLE THE SPONGE AND STRAWBERRY JUICE
Cut off the dry ends of the sponge to leave a rectangle. Use a whisk to loosen up the chilled pastry cream, then spread out over ¾ of the sponge and roll up (use a cloth or sheet of baking paper if required). Wrap the sponge in cling film and refrigerate for 5–6 hours before slicing.
Process half of the strawberries along with the sugar, milk and lemon. Finely chop the rest of the strawberries and mix into the juice.

Finishing

Divide the strawberry juice between 6 deep dishes and top with a generous slice of vanilla Swiss roll.

MENUS

AUTUMN

September | October | November

AUTUMN

MENU
25

| *page 174* |

Cream of pumpkin soup with coconut milk

Cod steak with plankton
and plain vegetables

Lemon drizzle cake
with candied red pepper and prunes

AUTUMN

MENU
26

| *page 180* |

Burnt onion consommé
with Macau artichoke
and Mimolette

Duck magret
with diced squash and black sesame seeds

Flat choux buns
with easy peanut cream

AUTUMN

MENU
27

| *page 186* |

Oysters in their shells
with sardine rillette,
ginger and frosted banana

Pan-fried squid
with Puy green lentil hummus
and bean sprouts

Coffee-flavoured jelly with
orange, white rum and limoncello granita

AUTUMN

MENU

28

| *page 192* |

| STARTER | MAIN | DESSERT |

Green razor clams
with poached eggs
in chervil mayonnaise

Scallops in their shells
and black rice with Livarot cheese

Filo pastry with chestnut honey,
figs and blackcurrants, served with caramel ice cream

AUTUMN

MENU

29

| *page 198* |

| STARTER | MAIN | DESSERT |

Burrata squares with carrot juice,
fresh dates and Parma ham

Giant split pea gnocchi with porcini mushrooms

Mirabelle plums in brandy,
served with mini sablé biscuits and toasted gingerbread

AUTUMN

MENU

30

| *page 204* |

| STARTER | MAIN | DESSERT |

Mackerel fillets with cider vinegar
and grilled piquillo peppers

Pork roast with
compte of damson and boudin noir,
einkorn wheat and chorizo

Quince-stuffed lettuce
with pink praline crème anglaise

Serves 6

700 g pumpkin, peeled
and cut into chunks

700 ml fresh milk

400 g coconut milk

½ kaffir lime leaf

120 g lightly salted whipped cream

40 g shredded coconut

Fine salt

PREPARATION TIME | *25 minutes*

COOKING TIME | *25–30 minutes*

Cream of pumpkin soup
with coconut milk

Method

1 TO COOK THE PUMPKIN
Cook the pumpkin from cold in lightly salted milk. Once boiling, add the coconut milk and kaffir lime leaf, then continue simmering for a further 15–20 minutes. Remove the kaffir lime leaf and process the mixture in a blender to a perfectly smooth, creamy soup.

2 FOR THE WHIPPED CREAM
Carefully fold the whipped cream into the grated coconut.

Finishing

Serve the pumpkin soup in soup bowls. Each guest can serve their own coconut cream on top of the hot soup.

Serves 6

6 x 120–140 g skinless cod steaks

2 tsp powdered plankton
(found in organic shops)

3 carrots, washed, peeled
and sliced diagonally

3 large turnips, washed, peeled
and quartered

2 tomatoes, peeled,
seeds removed, diced

1 small courgette, sliced

100 g fresh butter

Juice of ½ lemon

12 radishes, finely sliced and stored in an
ice bath

Fine salt

Sumac

PREPARATION TIME | *30 minutes*

COOKING TIME | *10–15 minutes*

Cod steak
with plankton and plain vegetables

Method

1 **FOR THE VEGETABLES**
Boil the carrots and turnips in salted water, then cool in cold water. Combine the carrots and turnips with the tomatoes and heat with a knob of butter and a few drops of water. Quickly sauté the courgette slices in a frying pan with the butter, (not long enough that they lose their crunch) and season with salt and sumac.

2 **TO COOK THE COD**
Season the cod steaks with salt. Cook for 4–5 minutes in sizzling butter, then turn over, add the plankton and cook for a further 5–7 minutes, basting continuously with a spoon. The fish should not brown but acquire a green hue.
Remove the fish from the pan and keep warm. Combine the cooking butter with the lemon juice.

Finishing

Place the cod steaks in the centre of each plate, then divide the vegetables evenly, creating a balance between raw and cooked, hot and cold. Drizzle with a little plankton butter.

AUTUMN

MENU
25

DESSERT

Serves 6

For the lemon drizzle cake

6 egg yolks

210 g sugar

Grated zest of 1 unwaxed lemon

100 g double cream

160 g flour

5 g baking powder

60 g candied lemon
(ready-made)

60 g melted butter, still warm and fluid

For the syrup

150 ml still mineral water

100 g sugar

60 ml freshly-squeezed lemon juice,
strained

For the candied red pepper

3 red peppers, peeled and finely diced

Sugar (the same weight as the pepper)

½ unwaxed lemon, finely sliced

Still mineral water

12 pitted prunes

PREPARATION TIME | *25 minutes*

COOKING TIME | *1 hour 30 minutes –
2 hours 25 minutes*

Lemon drizzle cake
with candied red pepper and prunes

Method

1 FOR THE CAKE
Preheat the oven to 180°C, 350°F, gas 4. Beat the egg yolks and sugar together until the mixture turns pale, then combine with the zest and cream. Mix in the butter, baking powder and candied lemon, then combine with the yolk mixture and finish with the melted butter.
Transfer to a 450 g non-stick loaf tin, filling to ¾ of its height, and bake for approximately 25 minutes (use the tip of a knife to check if it is ready). Let stand in the cake tin for 15 minutes before removing.

2 FOR THE LEMON SYRUP
Place the water, sugar and lemon juice in a saucepan and bring to the boil and simmer gently for 10 minutes. Next, drizzle over the cake little by little (the cake should absorb all of the syrup).

3 FOR THE CANDIED RED PEPPER
Weigh the diced red pepper, then add the same weight of sugar. Place the pepper, sugar and lemon slices in a saucepan, add water until fully submerged, then cover with baking paper and simmer gently for 2 hours (add a little more water if necessary). Add the prunes and leave to soak for a further 30 minutes. Remove from the heat and leave to cool completely.

Finishing

Serve the pepper and prunes in dessert bowls. Slice the cake and serve on a platter in the centre of the table. This dessert can be accompanied by a lemon granita or panna cotta.

AUTUMN

MENU
26

STARTER

Serves 6

4 onions, finely chopped

30 g butter

2 cloves garlic, chopped

1 sprig thyme

1 bay leaf

200 ml dry white wine (sauvignon blanc)

800 ml still mineral water

½ bouillon cube

1 tbsp wholegrain mustard

1 tbsp chives, chopped

4 x 1 cm-thick onion slices
   (1 large onion)

3 large Macau artichoke hearts,
   cooked in lemon-scented water
   (or 3 whole cooked artichokes,
   leaves and choke removed)

150 g Mimolette cheese,
   sliced using a peeler

Fine salt and freshly ground black pepper

Grilled baguette slices (to serve)

PREPARATION TIME | *20 minutes*

COOKING TIME | *30 minutes*

Burnt onion consommé
with Macau artichoke and Mimolette

Method

1 FOR THE CONSOMMÉ
Brown the onions in the butter without seasoning. Add the garlic, thyme and bay leaf, then pour in the white wine and reduce by ¾. Add the water and the bouillon cube, then simmer for approximately 30 minutes. Strain the stock. Remove the thyme and the bay leaf from the onions, then leave to cool and add the mustard and chives. Set aside.

2 FOR THE ONION SLICES
Use the oven's grill function to grill the onion slices. Add to the hot stock, then cover and infuse for approximately 30 minutes. Strain again, then adjust the seasoning to taste.

3 FOR THE ARTICHOKE HEARTS
Chop the artichoke hearts and bake in the oven at 150°C, 300°F, gas 2 for 5 minutes with a little stock.

Finishing

Divide the artichoke hearts between 6 warmed bowls and scatter with slices of Mimolette. Pour over the piping-hot consommé at the table. Serve the onions with mustard and chives separately, as a sauce, with grilled slices of baguette.

AUTUMN

MENU
26

MAIN

Serves 6

5 duck magrets (breast meat)

70 g brown sugar

120 g frozen blackcurrants

40 ml sherry vinegar

250 ml duck jus

3 g cornflour

600 g squash, cut into small dice

50 g fresh butter

2 tbsp black sesame seeds

Still mineral water

Fine salt and freshly ground white pepper

PREPARATION TIME | *20 minutes*

COOKING TIME | *30 minutes*

Duck magret
with diced squash and black sesame seeds

Method

1 TO COOK THE MAGRETS
Remove any excess fat from the magrets, score the skin and season with salt. Place skin-side down on a hotplate to melt the fat (7–8 minutes), then turn over to finish cooking (5–6 minutes). Remove and wrap in aluminium foil to allow the meat to rest.

2 FOR THE SAUCE
Prepare a caramel sauce with the brown sugar and a little water. Remove from the heat, add the blackcurrants and sherry vinegar and combine. Next, add the duck jus and simmer for 15 minutes over a low heat. Adjust the seasoning as required, then thicken the sauce using the cornflour.

3 FOR THE DICED SQUASH
Melt the butter in a fairly large saucepan, then add the squash, a little salt and water, then mix and cover with baking paper. Cook for 7–10 minutes, stirring regularly, until tender. Add the black sesame seeds at the end of cooking.

Finishing

Serve the sliced magrets on a platter in the centre of the table. Serve the diced squash on the plates and the sauce separately.

AUTUMN

MENU
26

DESSERT

Serves 6

For the choux pastry
150 g milk
5 g salt
10 g granulated sugar
150 g still mineral water
120 g fresh butter
180 g T55 flour
4 eggs
Icing sugar

For the easy cream
4 egg yolks
80 g sugar
25 g flour
180 g milk
10 ml golden rum
60 g fresh butter
20 g peanut butter
50 g peanuts, shelled, peeled and toasted
250 ml whipped cream

PREPARATION TIME | *30 minutes*

COOKING TIME | *50 minutes*

Flat choux buns
with easy peanut cream

Method

1 FOR THE FLAT CHOUX BUNS
Preheat the oven to 180°C, 350°F, gas 4. Place the milk, water, salt, sugar and butter in a fairly large saucepan and bring to the boil. Remove from the heat and add the flour all at once, then mix well with a spatula. Return to the heat, then work the dough with the spatula for 5–6 minutes until it stops sticking to the pan (you can also test it with a fingertip). Transfer to a mixing bowl, then add the eggs one by one while the dough is still hot. Transfer the choux pastry dough to a piping bag fitted with a smooth 8 mm nozzle. Pipe 6 x spiral shapes, each 7–8 cm in diameter, onto a baking sheet. Sandwich between another baking sheet, separated by wedges at a height of 3–4 cm, and bake for 15 minutes. Open the oven to release the vapour, then close again and bake for around 20 minutes more. Remove from the oven and transfer to a cooling rack.

2 FOR THE EASY CREAM
Beat together the egg yolks and sugar in a large mixing bowl until the mixture turns pale. Add the flour. Bring the milk to the boil, then pour over the yolks in a thin stream, stirring constantly, until the cream thickens. Transfer to a clean bowl and add the rum, fresh butter and peanut butter. Cover with food wrap and leave to cool before refrigerating. Just before serving, whisk the cream to loosen it and combine with the peanuts and the sweetened whipped cream.

Finishing

Place the warm, flat discs of choux pastry on 6 plates and dust generously with icing sugar. Serve the peanut cream separately.
This dish can be accompanied by a little pear ice cream or gingerbread.

AUTUMN

MENU

27

STARTER

Serves 6

½ banana, not too ripe, peeled and finely sliced

1 tin of 6 sardines in oil

1 tbsp shallot, chopped

1 tbsp chives, chopped

Juice of ½ lemon

Espelette pepper

1 tbsp vodka

36 deep no. 2 calibre oysters, shucked, removed from their shells and chilled (wash and chill the shells as well)

30 g fresh ginger, cut into very fine brunoise

Kelp

Toasted bread

Ketchup (optional)

PREPARATION TIME | *15 minutes*   COOKING TIME | *1 hour*

Oysters in their shells
with sardine rillette, ginger and frosted banana

Method

1 **FOR THE FROSTED BANANA**
Spread out the banana slices on baking paper and leave in the freezer for 1 hour.

2 **FOR THE SARDINE RILLETTE**
Use a fork to crush the sardines with the shallot and the chives. Season with lemon, Espelette pepper and vodka.

Finishing

Place 1 tsp rillette in each oyster shell. Divide the ginger and the banana slices between the oysters, placing them on top of the rillette inside the shell. Place the oysters in a large dish filled with ice and kelp. Serve with toast or even some ketchup, if desired.

MENU
27

MAIN

Serves 6

300 g Puy green lentils

60 g smoked bacon (in a single piece)

1 small bouquet garni

150 ml olive oil

180 g bean sprouts

20 ml walnut oil

Soy sauce

600 g squid, cleaned and sliced

Salt

PREPARATION TIME | *20 minutes*

COOKING TIME | *20–30 minutes*

Pan-fried squid
with Puy green lentil hummus and bean sprouts

Method

1 FOR THE LENTIL HUMMUS
Cook the lentils in lightly salted water with the smoked bacon and the bouquet garni, then drain, reserving the cooking liquid. Remove the bacon and dice. Discard the bouquet garni. Process the lentils to a purée, adding 110 ml olive oil. Loosen with a little cooking liquid if necessary to produce a smooth purée, then add the bacon lardons.

2 FOR THE FRESH SOYA
Just before serving, season the bean sprouts with the soy sauce and walnut oil.

3 FOR THE SQUID
Griddle the squid rings with the remaining olive oil.

Finishing

Divide the lentil hummus between the dishes, then top with the squid and place a bouquet of bean sprouts in the middle of the plate.

Serves 6

For the coffee–flavoured jelly

500 ml coffee

6 g gelatine leaves,
 soaked in cold water

60 g granulated cane sugar

Peel of 3 oranges,
 removed using a peeler

For the orange granita

500 ml freshly–squeezed orange juice,
 strained

120 ml limoncello

50 ml white rum

160 g granulated sugar

1 pear, peeled and diced

2 oranges, supremed, with each segment
 cut into thirds

PREPARATION TIME | *20 minutes*

Coffee-flavoured jelly
with orange, white rum and limoncello granita

Method

1 FOR THE COFFEE-FLAVOURED JELLY
Wring out the gelatine and dissolve in the very hot coffee with the cane sugar. Add the orange peels and infuse, covered with cling film, until completely cool. Strain, then leave to set in the refrigerator.

2 FOR THE ORANGE GRANITA
Combine the orange juice with the limoncello and rum, then add the sugar and stir with a whisk until completely dissolved. Pour this liquid into a deep dish and refrigerate for 3–4 hours. Scrape the ice with a fork to make granita.

3 FOR THE FRUIT
Combine the diced pear and the orange segments cut into thirds.

Finishing

Break up the coffee jelly with a spoon and divide between 6 dessert bowls. Place the fruit on top and finish with the orange granita. This dessert can be served with ladyfingers or slices of fruit cake.

AUTUMN

MENU

28

STARTER

Serves 6

6 medium eggs
1 litre water
150 ml distilled (white) vinegar

300 g spinach leaves, cleaned and
    removed from their stalks
60 g butter
250 ml milk

600 g razor clams, cleaned to remove
    any sand
50 ml olive oil

For the chervil mayonnaise
2 egg yolks
20 g strong mustard
Fine salt and freshly ground white pepper
100 ml sunflower oil
Juice of 1 lemon
2 tbsp chervil, chopped
1 tsp flat-leaf parsley, chopped

PREPARATION TIME | *25 minutes*

COOKING TIME | *25 minutes*

Green razor clams
with poached eggs in chervil mayonnaise

Method

1 FOR THE POACHED EGGS
Bring the water to the boil, then add the vinegar and leave to simmer. Crack the eggs into the boiling water one by one and cook for 2–3 minutes. Remove from the water and cool immediately in an ice bath. Remove the ragged edges from the eggs to give a smooth, round shape.

2 FOR THE GREEN JUICE
Cook the spinach in salted water at a rolling boil. Cool in cold water, drain and squeeze to extract as much of the water as possible. Heat the butter in a saucepan until it turns brown, then remove from the heat and halt the cooking process by adding the cold milk. Process the spinach, gradually adding the milk and butter mixture until smooth, thick and sauce-like in texture.

3 FOR THE RAZOR CLAMS
Open the clams raw and remove the flesh (the cylindrical part in the centre of the shell). Sauté very quickly in a non-stick frying pan with the olive oil, then drain and leave to cool. Next, cut into small pieces, combine with the green juice and refrigerate.

4 FOR THE CHERVIL MAYONNAISE
Whisk the egg yolks together with the mustard, salt and pepper, gradually adding the sunflower oil. Finish by adding the lemon juice, chervil and parsley.

Finishing

Divide the razor clams between 6 plates, placing them in the centre. Coat the poached eggs in the chervil mayonnaise and place on top.

AUTUMN

MENU
28

MAIN

Serves 6

6 large whole scallops (shucked and
cleaned by the fishmonger, with the
scallop still attached to the shell)

For the onion cream

2 sweet Cévennes onions, chopped

100 g butter

200 ml craft cider

20 ml white balsamic vinegar

20 ml maple syrup

100 ml double cream

2 pinches hot Madras curry powder

For the black rice

2 shallots, chopped

300 g black venere rice

200 ml dry white wine (sauvignon blanc)

400 ml still mineral water

120 g Livarot cheese, sliced

Salt, freshly-ground black pepper
and fleur de sel

PREPARATION TIME | *30 minutes*

COOKING TIME | *1 hour – 1 hour 15
minutes*

Scallops in their shells
and black rice with Livarot cheese

Method

1 FOR THE ONION CREAM
Gently sauté the onions in 50 g butter but do not allow to brown. Add salt. Pour in the craft cider, then reduce for 40 minutes, adding the curry powder 10 minutes in. Next, add the balsamic vinegar, maple syrup and cream. Simmer for 10 minutes. Process the resulting mixture in a blender.

2 FOR THE BLACK RICE
Sweat the shallots in the remaining butter in a casserole dish, then add the black rice, stirring with a spoon to separate the pieces. Add the white wine and water.
Preheat the oven to 180°C, 350°F, gas 4. Season the rice with salt, return to the boil, cover with baking paper and place in the oven for approximately 45 minutes: black rice may cook faster or slower depending on its origin. Add more liquid during cooking if necessary.

Finishing

15 minutes before serving, preheat the oven to 240°C, 475°F, gas 9. Place 1 tablespoon of hot onion cream in the bottom of the scallop shells, without covering the scallop itself. Top the cream with the black rice and cover with slices of Livarot cheese (the scallop should still be visible). Season the scallop with a pinch of fleur de sel and some pepper, then bake for 3–4 minutes or just long enough to melt the cheese and warm the scallop. Serve the rest of the rice and the onion cream in the centre of the table.

AUTUMN

MENU
28

DESSERT

Serves 6

4 tbsp chestnut honey
60 g butter
1 pack filo pastry

300 g blackcurrants
100 g sugar
20 ml crème de cassis liqueur
12 figs, quartered
Icing sugar
Caramel ice cream

PREPARATION TIME | *30 minutes*

COOKING TIME | *25 minutes*

Filo pastry with chestnut honey,
figs and blackcurrants, served with caramel ice cream

Method

1 FOR THE FILO PASTRY
Preheat the oven to 180°C, 350°F, gas 4. Heat the honey and butter together until melted. Line 6 x 12 cm baking hoops with filo pastry, add a pinch of honey–butter mixture to each one and allow to soak in. Bake for 8–10 minutes until the filo pastry turns amber in colour. Remove from the baking hoops once out of the oven. Leave to cool at room temperature.

2 FOR THE BLACKCURRANTS
Heat the blackcurrants with the sugar in a saucepan until they burst (20 minutes), then remove from the heat and add the liqueur.

3 FOR THE FIGS
Sprinkle the fig quarters with icing sugar and set aside.

Finishing

Place the burst blackcurrants in the bottom of the dishes. Place the fig quarters on top, then cover with the filo pastry discs and finish with the caramel ice cream.

Serves 6

For the carrot juice
500 ml carrot juice
50 ml olive oil

For the burrata
250 g fresh burrata cheese
50 ml whole milk
3 gelatine leaves,
  soaked in cold water
Fine salt and Espelette pepper

24 fresh dates, pitted and halved
1 tbsp maple syrup
20 ml lemon juice
50 ml still mineral water
6 thin slices Parma ham, cut into pieces

PREPARATION TIME | *30 minutes*

COOKING TIME | *25 minutes*

Burrata squares
with carrot juice, fresh dates and Parma ham

Method

1 FOR THE CARROT JUICE (one day in advance)
Very slowly reduce the carrot juice by $^4/_5$, stirring with a wooden spoon. Emulsify the reduced juice with 20 ml olive oil, then season lightly.

2 FOR THE BURRATA SQUARES
Heat the milk and use a whisk to stir in the gelatine until dissolved, then add the burrata cheese to melt. Season with salt and Espelette pepper, then process the mixture and pour into a baking dish up to 1.5 cm in depth. Leave to set in the refrigerator for 2 hours, then cut into 6 equal-sized squares. Return to the refrigerator.

3 FOR THE DATES
Heat the remaining olive oil In a large baking dish and cook the dates for 7–8 minutes with the maple syrup, lemon juice and water. Leave to cool at room temperature.

Finishing

Place the burrata squares in the centre of the plates, drizzle the carrot juice on top, then add the dates and finally the slices of Parma ham, "ruffled" for extra volume.
This starter can be served with focaccia or brioche.

AUTUMN

MENU

29

MAIN

Serves 6

500 g very green split peas

1 x 100 g slice smoked bacon

100 g T55 flour

20 g potato starch

80 g Beaufort cheese, grated

1 egg + 1 yolk

100 g butter

300 g double cream

600 g cleaned porcini mushrooms, diced

1 shallot, chopped

1 tbsp flat-leaf parsley, chopped

Fine and coarse salt and white pepper

PREPARATION TIME | *40 minutes*

COOKING TIME | *1 hour 30 minutes*

Giant split pea gnocchi
with porcini mushrooms

Method

1 FOR THE SPLIT PEA PURÉE
Boil the split peas in the water with the smoked bacon (45 minutes – 1 hour). Drain, setting aside the bacon. Once the split peas are completely dried and still hot, press through a sieve using a spatula.

2 FOR THE GNOCCHI
Weigh out 300 g of the split pea purée (it should be completely dry) and place in a mixing bowl with the flour, starch and Beaufort cheese. Mix well, add the eggs and season. Use a spoon to form into gnocchi, then cook one by one in simmering salted water (they are cooked when they rise to the surface). Cool in an ice bath and drain on a cloth.

3 FOR THE SMOKED BACON CREAM
Cut the bacon into small pieces and brown in a frying pan with 20 g of the butter. Heat the cream and add the pieces of bacon, then reduce by ⅓ and season.

4 FOR THE PORCINI MUSHROOMS
Fry the mushrooms with the remaining butter and the shallot until they darken. Season at the end.

Finishing

Add the flat-leaf parsley to the smoked bacon cream, then divide between 6 deep dishes. Steam the gnocchi (or, failing this, place in a greased baking dish and reheat in the oven at 150°C, 300°F, gas 2) and place on top of the cream. Finish by scattering the mushrooms over the top. Fresh walnuts can be added if desired.

AUTUMN

MENU
29

DESSERT

Serves 6

500 g mirabelle plums, pitted

30 ml mirabelle plum brandy
(or substitute regular plum brandy)

150 g brown sugar

150 g butter, softened
(left out at room temperature)

75 g icing sugar

30 g egg yolk, hard boiled and
pressed through a sieve (1 egg yolk)

150 g flour

6 slices gingerbread

PREPARATION TIME | *30 minutes*

COOKING TIME | *20 minutes*

Mirabelle plums in brandy,
served with mini sablé biscuits and toasted gingerbread

Method

1 **FOR THE MIRABELLE PLUMS**
Pan-fry the plums with the brown sugar for 5–7 minutes, but do not overcook. Next, add the brandy to the hot pan, remove from the heat and refrigerate.

2 **FOR THE MINI SABLÉ BISCUITS**
Preheat the oven to 160°C, 325°F, gas 3. Combine the softened butter with the icing sugar, then add the egg yolk and the flour, combine and leave to rest in the refrigerator for 20 minutes. Use your hands to shape the dough into little balls, then place on a lined baking sheet and bake for 8–10 minutes. Leave to cool before handling.

3 **FOR THE GINGERBREAD**
Toast the gingerbread slices on both sides under the grill.

Finishing

Divide the plums in brandy between individual dessert bowls, then sprinkle generously with mini sablé biscuits. Serve the warm toasted gingerbread on the side or on top of the plums. This dessert can be accompanied by sweet whipped cream with cinnamon, or frozen yoghurt with honey.

Serves 6

6 mackerel, 200–300 g
    (filleted by the fishmonger)

400 ml still mineral water

200 ml white wine

Peel of 2 lemons, removed using a peeler

2 sprigs thyme

2 bay leaves

1 teabag or musling bag filled with ½ tsp
    coriander, ½ tsp black pepper and 1 clove

1 red onion, finely sliced

1 stick celery, peeled and chopped

2 cloves garlic, crushed

1 carrot, finely sliced

100 ml cider vinegar

100 ml olive oil

1 x 300 g jar piquillo peppers (drained,
    opened and seeds removed)

Salt and Espelette pepper

PREPARATION TIME | *25 minutes*

COOKING TIME | *15–20 minutes*

Mackerel fillets
with cider vinegar and grilled piquillo peppers

Method

1 FOR THE MACKEREL FILLETS
Dry the mackerel fillets on paper towels, season with the salt and Espelette pepper and leave for 30 minutes at room temperature.

2 FOR THE MARINADE
Lay out the mackerel fillets (flesh-side up) in a large, deep baking dish. Bring the water to the boil with the white wine, lemon peel, herbs (thyme and bay leaf) and the spice-filled teabag. Add the onion, celery, garlic and carrot, followed by the vinegar and 50 ml of the olive oil. Simmer for 10 minutes.
Pour this marinade over the fish (they should be fully submerged), then arrange the vegetables evenly between the fish. Leave to cool at room temperature, then cover with food wrap and refrigerate overnight.

3 FOR THE PIQUILLO PEPPERS
Pour the remaining olive oil over the piquillo peppers and cook one by one in a non-stick frying pan or, even better, a griddle pan.

Finishing

Remove the thyme, bay leaf, lemon peel and teabag from the dish and serve as-is alongside the vegetables. The piquillo peppers should be served warm in a separate dish. Consider serving with toast and a courgette salad.

MENU
30

MAIN

Serves 6

1.2–1.5 kg boneless pork loin, prepared for roasting by the butcher

80 g butter

40 ml sunflower oil

2 onions, diced

1 carrot, diced

3 cloves garlic, crushed

2 sprigs thyme

2 bay leaves

150 ml dry white wine

10 damsons, pitted and chopped

40 g butter

200 g boudin noir

200 g einkorn wheat

40 g butter

100 g chorizo, diced

Fine salt and freshly ground black pepper

PREPARATION TIME | *40 minutes*

COOKING TIME | *3 hours*

Pork roast
with compote of damson and boudin noir, einkorn wheat and chorizo

Method

1 TO COOK THE ROAST
Preheat the oven to 200°C, 400°F, gas 6. Season the meat with salt and pepper, then brown in a frying pan with half of the butter and oil.
Meanwhile, sweat the onions and carrot in a lidded casserole dish with the remaining oil and butter. Add the garlic and herbs (thyme and bay leaf), place the meat on top of this mixture and place in the oven with the lid off for 15 minutes.
Add the white wine and roast for a further 15 minutes. Cover, lower the temperature to 150°C, 300°F, gas 2 and roast for a further 40–50 minutes (adding a little water during cooking if necessary) until the vegetables are juicy and caramelised. Remove the roast, wrap in aluminium foil and let stand, keeping warm. Strain the juices through a chinois, pressing the vegetables firmly.

2 FOR THE COMPTE OF DAMSON AND BOUDIN NOIR
Cook the damsons in the butter over a low heat for around 10 minutes until soft. Cut the boudin into pieces and add, then cook for a further 10 minutes, stirring regularly.

3 FOR THE EINKORN WHEAT
Boil the einkorn wheat in lightly salted water (30–50 minutes, according to pack instructions). Drain well. Heat the butter until bubbling, then add the chorizo, pour over the einkorn wheat while still hot, and combine.

Finishing

Carve the meat into fairly thick slices, then serve on a platter, drizzled with their cooking juices. Serve the einkorn wheat in individual bowls and place 1 heaped tablespoon of damson and boudin noir compote on each plate.

AUTUMN

MENU
30

DESSERT

Serves 6

For the quince jam

3 very yellow quinces, peeled,
   quartered and seeds removed
   and reserved along with the skins

1 litre still mineral water

350 g sugar

Peel of 4 lemons, removed using a peeler

1 vanilla pod, halved

For the stuffed lettuce

6 large, very green lettuce leaves

For the crème anglaise

4 egg yolks

80 g sugar

500 ml whole milk

100 g pink pralines, crushed

PREPARATION TIME | *30 minutes*   COOKING TIME | *1 hour 30 minutes – 2 hours 40 minutes*

Quince-stuffed lettuce
with pink praline crème anglaise

> ### Method

1 FOR THE QUINCE JAM
Wrap the quince seeds and skins in muslin. Place the water, lemon peels and vanilla in a pan and bring to the boil. Add the quince segments and the muslin bag. Cover with baking paper and leave to cook for 1½–2 hours: they are cooked when they can be pierced easily with the tip of a knife.
Process half of the hot quinces to a purée, then refrigerate immediately. Cut the rest into pieces and reserve in the cooking syrup.

2 FOR THE STUFFED LETTUCE
Boil the lettuce leaves for 1 minute, then cool in an ice bath. Spread out on a cloth, then gently cut off the edges with a knife.
Place the equivalent of one tablespoon of quince purée on each lettuce leaf and wrap up into balls. Drizzle with the cold quince cooking syrup and refrigerate.

3 FOR THE PRALINE CRÈME ANGLAISE
Whisk the egg yolks and sugar until the mixture turns pale. Bring the milk to the boil and add, stirring, to the mixture. Return to a low heat, stirring constantly, until the cream is thick enough to coat the spatula (but without ever allowing to boil). Strain through a chinois, then add the praline, combine and leave to cool completely.

> ### Finishing

Divide the praline crème anglaise between 6 deep dishes, then sprinkle over the drained quince pieces. Place a stuffed lettuce leaf in the centre of each dish.

APPENDICES

II

Merci
à les équipes
qui défendent
notre projet
dan le monde . . . .

Pi Gagnaire

Recipe index

Recipe index

Published in 2016 by
Grub Street
4 Rainham Close
London
SW11 6SS
Email:food@grubstreet.co.uk
Twitter: @grub_street
Facebook: Grub Street Publishing
Web: www.grubstreet.co.uk

Photography: Point 4
Editing: Anne Dolamore

A CIP record for this book is available from the British Library

ISBN 978-1-910690-31-4

Printed and bound in Slovenia